T0051756

Making Money Work for Us

Making Money Work for Us

How MMT Can Save America

L. Randall Wray

polity

Copyright © L. Randall Wray 2022

The right of L. Randall Wray to be identified as Author of this Work has been asserted in accordance with the UK Copyright, Designs and Patents Act 1988.

First published in 2022 by Polity Press

Polity Press
65 Bridge Street
Cambridge CB2 1UR, UK

Polity Press
111 River Street
Hoboken, NJ 07030, USA

All rights reserved. Except for the quotation of short passages for the purpose of criticism and review, no part of this publication may be reproduced, stored in a retrieval system or transmitted, in any form or by any means, electronic, mechanical, photocopying, recording or otherwise, without the prior permission of the publisher.

ISBN-13: 978-1-5095-5425-6
ISBN-13: 978-1-5095-5426-3 (pb)

A catalogue record for this book is available from the British Library.

Library of Congress Control Number: 2022933265

Typeset in 11 on 13pt Sabon
by Cheshire Typesetting Ltd, Cuddington, Cheshire
Printed and bound in the UK by CPI Group (UK) Ltd, Croydon

The publisher has used its best endeavors to ensure that the URLs for external websites referred to in this book are correct and active at the time of going to press. However, the publisher has no responsibility for the websites and can make no guarantee that a site will remain live or that the content is or will remain appropriate.

Every effort has been made to trace all copyright holders, but if any have been overlooked the publisher will be pleased to include any necessary credits in any subsequent reprint or edition.

For further information on Polity, visit our website:
politybooks.com

Contents

Acknowledgments

I would like to thank Dimitri Papadimitriou and the Levy Economics Institute for support over the past three decades; my current colleagues at Bard College, especially Pavlina Tcherneva; my former colleagues and students at the University of Missouri–Kansas City, including Mat Forstater, Stephanie Kelton, Jim Sturgeon, Bill Black, Yeva Nersisyan, and Eric Tymoigne; my wife, Xinhua, and kids Shane, Alina, and Allison; and – finally – my comrades in arms, Bill Mitchell and Warren Mosler. Above all, I want to recognize my indebtedness to my mentor for forty years, the late John Henry, and to Hyman Minsky, the greatest American economist of the second half of the twentieth century – on whose shoulders I stand.

Preface

I studied with Hyman Minsky in the early 1980s when he was writing his famous 1986 book (*Stabilizing an Unstable Economy*[1]). There are two phrases in that book that I remember him saying in class:

> Everyone can create money; the problem is to get it accepted.

> The need to pay taxes means that people work and produce in order to get that in which taxes can be paid.

The first of these has to do with the creation of money – by anyone – while the second concerns why anyone would want it.

Most of my work on money for the first decade after my PhD studies concerned the first statement. It is largely about the private money system; government enters primarily as a regulator of banks and through its central bank as the provider of bank reserves. We can call that the credit money system – how private money is created when banks make loans. My first book, *Money and Credit in Capitalist Economies* (1990[2]), went through all of that, and I've continued work in that area as I examined the causes of the 1980s thrift crisis and later the 2007 collapse of the global financial system – what Minsky called money manager capitalism, analyzed in my later book, *Why Minsky Matters* (2015[3]).

However, I never forgot the other point he made: we work hard to get the *government's* money because we have to pay taxes. That had led me to the J. M. Keynes of the *Treatise on Money*[4] and to G. F. Knapp's *State Theory of Money*[5] when I was writing my PhD dissertation in Bologna, Italy, in 1986.

I included a section on chartalism or the *state money* approach in the 1990 book, but it was brief since I was focusing on the role of credit money in the private sector. However, in the mid-1990s I returned to the role of the state in our monetary system, and discovered what I believe to be the best two articles ever written on money, by A. Mitchell Innes in 1913 and 1914. Keynes had reviewed the first one and aside from some quibbles he declared it to be correct. Unfortunately, these articles were largely forgotten until I republished them in my 2004 book, *Credit and State Theories of Money*.[6]

What struck me is that Innes was able to integrate a state money approach and a credit money approach. To understand our money, what Keynes called "modern money," you must have both. Otherwise, to borrow a metaphor, you've got Hamlet without the Prince.

A group of us first at the Levy Institute in New York and then at the University of Missouri–Kansas City (but also including others, especially Warren Mosler, Bill Mitchell, and Charles Goodhart) dug deeper into this and gradually developed what is now called Modern Money Theory (MMT). My 1998 book, *Understanding Modern Money*,[7] was the first academic exposition of the approach, which was simplified in my "primer" of 2012.[8]

MMT has been in the news constantly since 2019 – at first derided as dangerous "crazy talk," and then embraced as governments ramped up spending to deal with the global COVID-19 pandemic.

Many think we claim to have invented some stand-alone, entirely new, approach to money. That is false. We stand on *the shoulders of giants* (the third phrase I recall from Minsky) – there is really no completely new theory in Modern Money Theory; MMT is an integration, one that integrates those two phrases from Minsky. We argue that this integration provides a new framework for analyzing monetary and fiscal policy in what we call sovereign currency nations. That framework is developed in detail in our MMT-based textbook, *Macroeconomics*.[9]

Over the past twenty-five years we have investigated all the details important to answering the question: "How does the sovereign government really spend?" While I'm sure there were economists in both the Federal Reserve Bank (Fed) and the US Treasury who understood all the operational details, these were not understood in academia or policy circles.

They mostly still are not.

But MMT has taken off; indeed, it has taken on a life of its own in the blogosphere. It is loved by many and perhaps hated by more. This current book is positioned in between the primer and an academic text, for those who already know the basics of MMT but who want to dig a bit deeper.

One of my graduate students in my class on money, who happened to be much older than the others, had to make a presentation at the end of the semester. He brought in a bag of those funny glasses that distort your vision. He asked everyone to don a pair and then began his talk. He discussed how the world had looked to him before he started the class on money – it looked just like the world looked to us now, with those funny glasses on: distorted. We looked at a fuzzy and barely comprehensible world with our impaired vision. He then proclaimed that we should take them off and look at the world anew! As we did, he told us we'd never see the world in the same way again – and that is precisely the way he felt after discovering Modern Money Theory. All those old cobwebs that had distorted his vision had been cleared away and he was ready to see the monetary world as it actually exists.

Your results may be similar.

An Introduction to Modern Money Theory

Modern Money Theory (MMT) provides a description of the way money actually works in our modern world. Money is a scary topic. It is also rather complex. So bear with me.

We will begin with a discussion of what we might call the "nature" of money – what *is* this thing we call money? When we use the term, most people will think of a shiny coin or a paper "note" or "bill" – something they can get their hands on to buy something they want. But today the vast majority of payments do not involve use of coins or notes.

Some will also think of an idealized past, when money was "backed up" by "hard" gold or silver, giving it a "real" value. They bemoan our modern money that appears to have no real or permanent value – what many call a "fiat currency." Some even heed the call of the Ron Pauls of the world to bring back the gold standard.

And since the global economy nearly collapsed in the late "aughts" of the beginning of the twenty-first century, many – rightly – think there is something wrong with money. They want to reform our monetary system.

But if we are going to reform it, we really need to understand it.

This book will help you to understand both our private money and our government money: what money really is, where it comes from, and how it works. Along the way, we'll see how this alternative perspective sheds light on reform – how we could change the monetary system to make it work better for *us*. This requires sweeping away mountains of misunderstanding about money.

A. MMT's Shocking Conclusions

MMT reaches conclusions that are shocking to many who've been taught the conventional wisdom. Most importantly, it challenges the orthodox views about government finance, monetary policy, the so-called inflation–unemployment trade-off, the wisdom of fixed exchange rates, and the folly of striving for current account surpluses. (If you don't know about any of those things, don't worry – indeed that might make it easier to follow what comes!)

For most people, the greatest challenge is MMT's claim that a sovereign government's finances are nothing like those of households and firms. While we hear all the time the statement that "if I ran my household budget the way that the federal government runs its budget, I'd go broke," followed by the claim "therefore, we need to get the government deficit under control," MMT argues this is a false analogy.

Of course, households and firms can and do become insolvent when they issue too much debt. But a sovereign, currency-issuing government is *nothing* like a currency-using household or firm. The sovereign government cannot become insolvent in its own currency; it can always make all payments as they come due in its own currency.

Governments spend first, then tax. That means tax revenue is not needed for spending. That does not mean taxes are unimportant – they serve other useful purposes. But the national government does not need to receive its own currency before it can spend – indeed, it cannot receive currency until after it spends.

Another conclusion is that a sovereign government does not need to "borrow" its own currency in order to spend. Indeed, it cannot borrow currency that it has not already spent!

This is why MMT sees the sale of government bonds by the sovereign as something quite different from borrowing: bond sales are part of monetary policy and help the central bank to manage interest rates. Governments don't need to borrow their own currency! As we will explain, governments spend their currency first and then receive it back in tax payment.

We'll revisit this argument later. What is important for now is MMT's recognition that government's spending is never constrained by taxes or by "bond market vigilantes" who might refuse to lend. To put it as simply as possible, governments today spend by "keystrokes" that they cannot ever run out of.

It surprises most people to hear that banks operate in a similar manner. They lend their own deposits into existence and accept them in payments on loans they hold. Strange, but true!

A century ago, a bank would issue its own bank notes when it made a loan. The debtor would repay loans by redeeming bank notes. Obviously, banks had to create the notes before debtors could pay down debts using the bank notes.

However, banks gradually got out of the business of issuing notes and instead turned to deposit banking. In the US today, only the Federal Reserve Bank (the government's bank) issues notes – our green paper currency. Private banks only issue deposits.

Banks now create deposits (not notes) when they make loans; debtors repay those loans using bank deposits (and the deposits of any US bank can be used to pay down loans at any other US bank). Almost all bank loans are repaid this way – by debiting bank deposits. And what this means is that banks need to create the deposits first before borrowers can repay their loans.

Hence, there is a symmetry: the sovereign spends currency (or central bank reserves – explained later) into existence first, and then taxpayers use the currency (or central bank reserves) to pay taxes; and banks lend their deposits into existence, then the bank's debtors use bank deposits to pay down loans.

The money is always created "out of thin air" – when the government spends or the banks lend. There's no theoretical limit to the government's ability to create its money (currency and reserves) and no limit to banks' ability to create bank money (deposits). You may find that shocking, and maybe even scary. This book will explain how money creation works and how we can use that knowledge to improve the functioning of our economy.

We will argue that the true constraints we face are real resource constraints and the limits of our knowledge. If we know how to do something, and we have the real resources (labor, natural resources, and productive capacity) required, we can find a way to afford to do it. If we have unemployed resources (most importantly labor), we can find a way to pay that labor to work. If we have idle plant and equipment, we can find the finances to put it to work, too. Importantly, if we have the resources and technology required to save the planet from climate catastrophe, we can financially afford to do it.

This does not mean government faces no constraints – it faces political constraints as well as real resource constraints. Even if politicians did not worry about "where will the money come from," they do care what money is spent on – that is, they have preferences regarding what the government should do. Further, policy often would lead to competition between the government and the private sector over use of resources. Even if there are a lot of unemployed workers and machines, it can be difficult to ensure that a new policy would not also demand resources that are already in use. In that case, the government would bid against private use of those resources. In other words, there could be a real trade-off: less private use and more public use. Since government doesn't face a financial constraint similar to that faced by the private sector (and the private sector needs to make a profit, the government doesn't), the government can win a bidding war. Not only does the government end up with the resources, the bidding war causes prices to rise. The result could be inflation.

Still, the usual situation (outside major wars) is that there are unemployed resources that could be mobilized for public programs. And if the government can surmount the political constraints, it can always afford to mobilize the unemployed resources in the public interest. Money is not the problem.

Ultimately, this should be comforting, not scary. Understanding how money really works lets us focus on the real barriers – politics, real resources, technical know-how, and inflation. In coming years we face a number of challenges – one might even claim we face existential threats perhaps greater than humans have had to deal with since they first came out of Africa. Survival of anything like organized human civilization may be in question. But the scientists claim that we have most of the know-how to tackle the challenges. MMT claims that we have the financial ability – we can finance what it takes to rise to the challenge. If we can clear away the misunderstandings, align the politics, and mobilize the resources, we can win.

We hope that this book will motivate you to pressure those with the power to take action to do what is necessary to make the world a safer and better place for humanity.

B. Themes to Be Covered

This book will provide an overview of several themes that are important to Modern Money Theory:

- What is the nature of money?
- How does private money get into the economy?
- How does the government's own money get into the economy?
- How does the government really spend?
- Can a government be forced into bankruptcy by the weight of its own debt?
- What are the true constraints we face?
- What are the trade-offs?
- Is it true that economics is a zero-sum game?
- What role does money creation play in creating financial crises?
- What can we do to promote economic and financial stability?

These issues will be developed in more detail throughout the first four chapters of the book. In chapter 1 we examine what we mean by the term "money"; in chapter 2 we look at how money gets into the economy. Chapter 3 examines whether we can have "too much money" – that is, so much that prices rise rapidly. In chapter 4 we develop an understanding of monetary "balance."

In the second half of the book, we tackle policy issues. Chapter 5 looks at the trade-offs, zero-sum economics, and potential free lunches available to policy makers. Chapter 6 looks at how we can frame issues surrounding money. Money can be a scary topic for both policy makers and the public. We need to provide a proper framing to support our desire for policy that serves the public interest.

Chapter 7 details the MMT approach to a variety of policy issues: government spending and taxing, inflation, and budget deficits. It examines the three policies that are fundamental to the MMT approach: the job guarantee to anchor the domestic value of the currency; interest rate targeting as the main tool for monetary policy; and a floating exchange rate to support domestic policy space. We close with a discussion of the state of play of MMT in Washington policy-making circles.

1
What Is Money?

A. Money Is What Money Does?

What is money? You will probably answer: "money is what I use to buy stuff."

That is a perfectly sensible answer, defining money by its function. We call this function "medium of exchange" – you *exchange* money for the stuff you want to buy.

After a few moments of thought, you will add: "I also use money to store value – so that I can buy stuff later." This refers to money as something you can hoard, although unlike Scrooge, you do plan to spend it, eventually – even if you are not sure what you'll buy. Holding money lets you postpone spending.

You also might offer that you use money to pay off your debts. We can call this function the "means of payment." Money can help you get out of debt.

You can also mention that we use money as a measuring unit, to calculate money (or "nominal"[1]) values: "I think that painting is worth a thousand dollars" or "I don't think it is worth it to pay $350 for a Taylor Swift concert." This is money functioning as a unit of account – sort of like using the yard or meter to measure length or the quart or liter to measure weight.

But let us go deeper. What *is* money? Can you describe what it is that you use to buy things, hoard value, and make payments on debts?

Your first thought will probably turn to paper money – the green dollar bill if you are in America, with George Washington on the front, signed by the US Treasurer and the Secretary of the Treasury. On the back it says "IN GOD WE TRUST" over the word ONE, and there's a curious picture of a pyramid with an eye at the top and some unintelligible (Latin) language.

After further inspection you find the words "THIS NOTE IS LEGAL TENDER FOR ALL DEBTS, PUBLIC AND PRIVATE," apparently confirming what you said earlier – you can pay your own (private) debts with it. (And also public debts – whatever that might mean! We'll investigate later.)

So, is money just paper? Well, certainly most paper is *not* money! And you will quickly add that not all money is *paper*. You've got a quarter in your pocket (interestingly, the US is unusual in that the largest denomination coin in common use – the quarter – has such a small value relative to that in most other developed nations). It is made of metal with a milled edge, has a picture of dear old George on the front, also trusts in God, and on the reverse side has either an eagle or, if of more recent vintage, a symbol from one of the fifty states. Is money metal? No, of course not – only these special stamped coins qualify as money – most metal, even valuable precious metal, is not money.

But what do you actually *spend* – just special pieces of paper or metal? After reflection, you note that most payments you make do not involve paper notes or metal. You use checks for many of your payments, writing a name (of a person or business entity) on the line that says "pay to the order of," then an amount, and finish with your signature. The recipient deposits your check in her bank, and your bank account is debited and hers is credited. Is that money? You can make purchases, store value, and pay down debt using checks – so checks certainly fulfill the functions of money.

Maybe the bank keeps a drawer with your name on it, filled with George Washington paper notes and metal quarters? When you write a check, maybe the bank takes money out of your drawer and puts it in the drawer of the recipient? *Hmmm. That must be a lot of work. Hundreds of millions of bank account drawers full of cash and perhaps trillions of transactions weekly – those bank gnomes must be very busy!* No, it doesn't work that way. You've probably had a peek inside your bank's vault – not nearly big enough to hold cash in an amount equal to all of the deposits of the bank's customers.

Increasingly you make payments online through electronic transfers, by providing long strings of mysterious numbers. Do banks take notes and coins out of your account and stuff them into the fiber-optic cables that link up all the computers so that they can flow to the right bank accounts? Obviously not – your computer keystrokes send instructions to the bank to make "electronic" payments for you. Are those photons that travel at the speed of light through the internet *money*? Is that what money *is*? A mere photon?

On final reflection you remember that many – maybe most – of your payments are made by submitting a (credit or debit) card to the merchant's card reader. *Is money plastic?* Or is there money somehow stored on your card and sucked out by the machine when you make a purchase? Not likely. But is this really money? You object that if you use a *credit* card, you still have to pay for the purchase later – usually through a debit to your bank account or by writing a check. But you do not pay the *store* – you make a payment to the *bank* that issued your card. That bank paid the merchant for you, and your bank makes a payment to the bank issuing the credit card when your account is debited or your check is presented for payment.

Not only is money scary but it is complicated, too! It is paper, it is metal, it is plastic, or . . . it is nothing but an ephemeral and quirky photon! Maybe approaching money from the perspective of the functions it serves is not the best way to do it, after all. It seems that lots of different "moneys" can be used to serve money's functions.

B. I Owe You, You Owe Me

Let's try to answer the question more directly: what *is* money? What do all these things (if we can call them such?) that function as money have in common? Those George Washington notes are issued by the central bank of the US, the Federal Reserve (Fed). Technically, they are "liabilities," or I Owe You's (IOUs), of the Fed. The demand deposits are liabilities of the banks. The credit card debt accepted by the merchant is an IOU of the bank that issued the card (and the merchant pays a fee – two or three percent of the purchase price for the "convenience" of letting you walk off with your purchases). And you, of course, owe the credit card issuer – your promise to pay is the asset of the bank that issued your card. You are likely to meet that promise using a debit from your demand deposit account at your bank – your asset, your bank's liability.

All of these entities are tied together through a network of IOUs. We don't want to get into complicated accounting now, but every economic entity (individual, household, firm, charitable organization, financial institution, and government) has a balance sheet (whether they know it or not!). We can think of this as a table with two columns that looks like a T (rather brilliantly, called a "T account"). We can label the left-hand side "assets" and the right-hand side "liabilities." The T accounts here just show the changes to balance sheets involved in a house purchase.

	You
Asset	Liability
+House	+Mortgage

Bank

Asset	Liability
+Mortgage	+Deposit

Seller

Asset	Liability
−House	
+Deposit	

For example, let's say you buy a house using a mortgage from your bank. We show your assets increasing by "+House" and your liability increasing by "+Mortgage." This is because you owe the mortgage debt and will make monthly payments. The bank's assets increase by the value of your mortgage (they loaned you the money to buy the house – since you owe them, that is their asset) and their liability has increased by the amount of the check used to purchase the house. Deposits are always the liability of the bank – the bank owes the depositor. What does the bank owe? The right of the depositor to make a withdrawal or to write a check against the deposit.

This deposit is now owned by the seller, so it shown up as "+Deposit" as an asset of the seller; however, the seller has lost a house so that is a negative entry – a deduction from assets (−House). Note we have kept this as simple as possible, ignoring other items on the balance sheets, ignoring the fact that you probably made a down payment (we assumed you obtained a mortgage loan for the full sales price), and assuming the house seller uses the same bank. All of these simplifying assumptions can be relaxed – but that merely complicates the exposition without changing anything important.

Since World War II, the standard US mortgage has had a fixed interest rate with a term of thirty years.[2] You sign a "note" promising that every month you will make a payment of $1,000, which includes interest and principal. On your balance sheet, the house is your asset and your note is your liability (your bank holds your *note* as its asset). Thirty years later, the Day of Redemption finally arrives when you make your last house payment. The bank returns your note and you invite all your neighbors over for a "note burning party."[3] Hallelujah!

The Fed's George Washington "note" is its liability. When it receives its own note back in payment, it might, too, have a "note burning party" (actually, the Fed shreds the notes and if you take a tour of one of the District banks, you can receive a bag of shredded notes as a souvenir). Or, if the note is in good shape, the Fed might store it for reissue later. However, when the note is in the Fed's storehouse it is not counted as a liability – it is just a scrap of paper.[4]

What about metallic coins? These are usually issued by the national treasury. In the US today, the Treasury only issues coins, although in the past it also issued paper notes. Like paper notes, coins are the liabilities of the issuer.[5] Treasuries also issue bills (very short-term debt, usually thirty days; we still call the green paper notes "dollar bills," indicating they are IOUs with a short term to maturity – in fact a maturity equal to zero) and issue bonds of various longer maturities (perhaps up to thirty years or even longer). These are also liabilities of the treasury but, unlike coins and paper notes, they promise to pay interest (like your mortgage note).

Earlier we discussed the use of bank accounts to make purchases. Your checking and savings accounts are your assets, but they are the liabilities of your bank. Banks typically issue two main types of deposit accounts: demand deposits (with funds available "on demand") and time deposits (banks can require notice before funds are withdrawn). Today banks pay interest on deposits (usually higher interest on time deposits than on demand deposits).[6] When you make payments by writing a check, by using a debit card, or through an electronic funds transfer, you are using bank liabilities. Your account is debited and the recipient of your payment gets a credit to her account, probably held at a different bank, and the Fed "clears" the accounts of the two banks. As mentioned, when you make payments using "plastic" (a credit card), the card-issuing bank makes the payment for you. You will then pay down your credit card debt by using your bank deposit (often held at a different bank). (Things are simpler if you use a debit card. Your bank simply debits your account and makes a payment for you – e.g. to the grocery store at which you shopped.)

Firms also use commercial banks to make payments for them – to purchase supplies and pay wages to their workers. Typically, commercial banks make short-term loans to firms for this purpose, crediting the checking account of the firm. This loan is counted as an asset of the bank, and as a liability of the firm. The firm's demand deposit is the bank's liability and the firm's asset. When the firm pays wages, its demand deposit is debited; the worker deposits her paycheck into her bank and receives a credit to her own checking account. (If she happens to use the same bank that the firm uses, the bank simply debits the firm's account and credits the worker's account. If she uses a different bank, the process is a bit more complicated, as reserve clearing is required.)

We could continue with other examples, but you have noticed that there is one thing all of these kinds of money have in common: they are liabilities of their issuer and assets of their holder. To recap: coins and notes are liabilities of the treasury or central bank that issued them and are assets of the person or entity that happens to hold them; bank deposits are liabilities of the banks that issued them, and assets of the depositors.

What about a savings deposit, or more generally, a time deposit (such as a ninety-day certificate of deposit)? Again, these are liabilities of the bank or thrift that issued them and assets of the holder. What about a corporate bond? It is a liability of the issuing corporation and an asset of the holder. A government bond? A liability of the government and asset of the owner. The firm's commercial loan is its liability and an asset of the bank. You get the picture: firms (financial and nonfinancial) issue liabilities that are held as financial assets by others.

Your credit card debt is the asset of the bank that issued your card and it is your liability. Your home mortgage is your liability and the asset of the bank, the financial institution, or – increasingly –the trust that securitized it.[7] Your car loan is your liability and an asset of the institution holding it (and, again, these are also increasingly securitized).

Do we want to call all of these things *money*? All of them have several things in common. They are liabilities of the issuer. They are *financial* assets of the holder. They have a value denominated in the *money of account* (US dollar in America, UK pound, Australian dollar, Japanese yen, and so on). There are other characteristics shared by some, but not all, of these liabilities.

Some of them (coins, paper notes, demand deposits, credit cards) can be used immediately to make payments; *some* of them require payment of interest (bonds, delayed payments on credit card debt, mortgages, commercial loans).

Some of them can be touched (coins and notes, checks), while many of them are just electronic entries on computerized balance sheets (credit card debts, commercial loans, most government bonds).

Maybe less obvious is that all of them share the characteristic that they can be *redeemed* in at least one of two senses. Let's see what those are by examining what we mean by the term "redemption."

C. Redemption

Let's deal with the most commonly used sense of the term, already alluded to above in the comment about

"Redemption Day." When you take out a mortgage, a car loan, or a student loan, you promise to make regular payments of interest and principal. You make these payments using liabilities – usually bank liabilities or "cash" (government liabilities). Note that you cannot simply use your own IOU to retire your IOU – this should be obvious. If you just wrote another IOU, you would still be in debt. However, if you had taken out the loan at your own bank, you can write a check on your account at that bank to pay the loan – using a "second party" IOU (the bank is the second party; you are the first). You cannot pay down a debt using your "first party" IOU – you'd still be in debt.

But most often you use a third party IOU – for example you write a check on your bank account (say, First Bank of Rhinebeck) to pay down your car loan debt owed to a different bank (say, GM Financial). So, normally you use a "third party" IOU – neither your own IOU (first party), nor the IOU of your creditor (second party) to pay down debt. Once you have made all the required payments, you are no longer in debt. You have "redeemed" your debt, and your "note" (mortgage note or car loan note) is returned to you for shredding or burning – or framing!

You have probably presented store coupons for "redemption," receiving a discounted price. When a store issues a coupon for a discount on hair spray (or a pizza restaurant issues a coupon for a free pizza), it is actually issuing a debt. It remains in debt until those coupons are presented for redemption, at which time they are destroyed. Of course, many or even most of the coupons never get submitted for redemption. Most have expiration dates, after which the issuers are no longer obligated to accept them (their "debt" is extinguished). The issuers expect this – if an issuer prints coupons with a nominal value of $100,000, the actual debt this represents in terms of discounted sales will only be a fraction of that value.

When you hold a liability – whether it is a coupon for a free pizza, a corporate bond, or even a US Treasury quarter – you are a creditor. You might not have ever thought about it that way but holding "money" (or any other financial asset) makes you the creditor of the issuer. As a creditor, you can return that liability to the issuer in "redemption." You "redeem" the coupon for a free pizza. That extinguishes your credit, or claim, for a free pizza. This also wipes out the debt of the pizza restaurant – they no longer owe you a pizza. The restaurant is "redeemed" of its debt, too.

There is another related use of the term "redemption." Many people still reminisce about the days long gone when it was possible to "redeem" a government's currency for gold. This is often referred to as "convertibility." For example, until President Nixon closed the "gold window" in 1971, the US promised to convert dollars to gold at an exchange rate of $35 to an ounce of gold. Interestingly, Americans were not allowed to "redeem" dollars for gold – only foreign holders of dollars could submit dollar liabilities (paper notes and reserves issued by the US Treasury and Fed) for redemption.[8] The dollars foreigners held were similar to the pizza coupons you might hold – and just as the pizza restaurant extinguishes its coupon debt in exchange for pizza, the US government extinguished its dollar debt in exchange for gold. This is what we mean when we define "redemption" as the return of a debt to the issuer, whether to claim a pizza or an ounce of gold.

Returning to the more common version of redemption, you might be simultaneously a creditor of your bank and a debtor to the bank – if for example you have a checking account and also a car loan from the bank. You can use the bank's liability (your demand deposit) to cancel your liability (car loan) to the bank. Note that here there are two acts of redemption: you are "redeemed" (you no longer owe the bank since you've paid off the car loan) and the bank is "redeemed" (it doesn't owe you the deposit you used to pay down your own debt).

The redemption is mutual and simultaneous. *Hallelujah!*

More generally, there is a principle of credit that has long been understood: if you owe someone, you can get out of debt by presenting your creditor's debt to cancel your own. Now imagine that there is some entity to which most of us owe debts – an entity that is the major creditor in the society. Let us also assume that this creditor has issued a lot of its own IOUs. By the general principle of redeemability just discussed, we can use the creditor's own IOUs to pay down our IOUs to the creditor. Since most of us owe that creditor, we all seek that creditor's IOUs so that we can use them to get out of debt. So long as the creditor keeps its own IOUs somewhat scarce relative to the debts it holds, it can ensure its IOUs are always in wide demand.

Further imagine that the government plays that role as the major creditor, with most of its citizens (or subjects under a monarch) in the position of owing taxes to the government. The population would want to obtain the government's IOUs in order to pay tax liabilities. In that case, the government could impose obligations on the population – making itself the creditor. The obligations would be payable in the government's own currency liabilities. It would spend the currency, accepted by the population because taxes could be paid with currency. The government would "redeem" the currency when received in payment of taxes. As we said before, both the taxpaying population and the government would be simultaneously redeemed. The currency received from taxes is burned, or melted, or warehoused for later use.

The American colonies (before the Revolution of 1776) understood this quite well.[9] Still under British rule, they were prohibited from coining money. And yet colonial governments needed money – for infrastructure like roads, and especially for military skirmishes against Native Americans, French, and Canadians.

Always short of British coins, they discovered that they could impose "redemption taxes" and issue paper notes that their populations would use to pay the tax. This was the first big use of paper money in the West (the Chinese had used it for a long time). Since their residents needed to pay the tax, they would accept the notes in payment by the colonial governments – to purchase supplies for the militias, for example. Adam Smith – the acknowledged "father" of economics – studied the American colonies and noted that some of them issued paper money notes (without gold backing) that maintained their value so long as the colonies did not issue too much.[10]

He went on to provide a hypothetical example – he said that a prince could issue paper money and that it would be accepted so long as his subjects could pay taxes with it. This is why every colonial act that authorized the issue of paper money also imposed a redemption tax. The tax was set to raise revenue more or less equal to the amount of currency that would be issued. So if you were the Governor of the Virginia Colony, you would impose a tax expected to raise 10,000 Virginia pounds, then print and spend 10,000 pounds of notes, to be collected at tax time. (The colonies used pounds; only after the Revolution did America switch to dollars – based on the Spanish currency of the time in a conscious snubbing of Britain.)

Most of the notes came back to the government when taxpayers paid their taxes. Some remained in circulation – about a quarter – and continued to be used in private transactions.

What did the government do with the tax revenue? Spend it? No. They burned it. All of it. They carefully kept records to show they burned all their revenue! Taxes are for redemption, not for revenue. Colonial governments did not need the revenue. They spent the currency into the economy, and taxed it back so they could burn it. The true purpose of the tax was to create a demand for the notes. Collecting taxes then ensured that both the government and those owing taxes "redeemed" themselves: taxpayers were "redeemed" as they no longer owed taxes, and the government was "redeemed" because its own debts – represented by the notes – were burned. The redemption was mutual and simultaneous.

This was not some strange colonial quirk. As we'll see,

history is littered with similar examples. Spend the currency into existence and then tax it back and destroy the revenue. Taxes are not for spending.

At the end of World War II, the Chairman of the Federal Reserve Bank of New York (the most important branch of the Federal Reserve System), Beardsley Ruml, said the same thing in a paper he titled "Taxes for revenue are obsolete."[11] While taxes might be important for other purposes (that we'll examine later), government doesn't need "revenue" in order to spend.

And it is clear that the American colonists understood this before 1776. It is written into the laws. The taxes were called *redemption taxes*, after all! The purpose of the tax was to collect the notes, redeeming them.

Keep this in mind: *Taxes are for redemption, not revenue.*

The term "redemption" has religious connotations – reflecting the historical origins of money in the early Babylonian temples over four millennia ago. Indebted sinners seek redemption. Those early priests invented a unit of account in which to record the debts of Babylonia's "sinners" – that is, the debtors. Those records of debt were kept on clay cuneiform tablets. Debtors could pay their way to redemption. More on that later, in chapter 4. The point is that money was created for use in record-keeping, and when debts were paid, the debtors were redeemed.

To sum up: taxes create a demand for money. That, in turn, gives value to the currency. By extrapolation, we could argue that today the US dollar has value not because it might be redeemable for gold (it isn't!) but because you must obtain dollars to pay taxes – to redeem yourselves in the eyes of the tax authorities. This is what Adam Smith meant when he said nonconvertible paper money will retain its value so long as you do not issue too much of it – relative to the redemption taxes.

We might ponder the question: must government run a balanced budget? Do the tax "revenues" have to equal the number of notes spent by government? No! Even in colonial America about 25 percent of the notes remained out in circulation. People preferred them to the British king's coins for use in commerce. Only about three-fourths of the notes were collected in tax payments – and then burned. So the issue of notes exceeded the receipt of notes in tax payments because the population wanted to keep some of them. The desire to save the currency ensures the government spends more paper money than it collects in taxes, enabling the population to save in the form of paper notes.

Hold that thought. Later we will examine why it is perfectly normal for the government to spend more than it taxes – what we call a deficit. The deficit results because the population wants to accumulate the government's debt as saving. By spending more than its revenue, the government lets us spend less than our income – what we call "saving."

The mechanism of imposing redemption taxes to drive a currency was not a new discovery by the colonial governments. For many hundreds of years before, European monarchs and other authorities (including religious authorities and feudal lords) had imposed obligations on subjects in the form of fees, fines, taxes, rent, tribute, and tithes. They then issued their own debts in purchases of supplies (or labor), and received them back in payment of those obligations.

D. Record-Keeping in Money

Throughout the Middle Ages, a common currency used in Britain was the wooden tally stick.[12] What governments used for spending and taxing was mostly *not* coins, but pieces of hazelwood sticks. The king's exchequer (treasurer) would first notch the stick to indicate the nominal amount (a larger notch would indicate a larger value) and then split it lengthwise to produce a "stock" and a "stub". The creditor would retain the stock while the debtor would take the stub (to ensure the stock was not tampered with by adding more notches to increase the value).[13] These terms, stock and stub are still used in English for rock concert tickets and baseball games. And shares sold on Wall Street are still called stocks – evidence of an equity claim against the issuing firm.

Why would anyone accept a wooden stick in payment? Because obligations to the crown were paid by delivering half of the tally back to the treasury, which would match stock and stub to make sure no one was counterfeiting. If they matched, taxes were paid.

Any obligation can drive money. It didn't have to be taxes – it could be fees, fines, tribute, or religious tithes. One uses money for redemption – to remove the obligation. Hallelujah! Free (of debt) at last!

What is the tally stick or the paper note or the gold coin? It is the record of the issuer's IOU – the issuer's debt or obligation. That record of the IOU is returned to the issuer in payment. This is what we can call the fundamental law of credit: the issuer of an IOU must take it back in payment. If you refuse your own IOU, you are defaulting on that promise of redemption.[14]

When the debtor retired her debt, the two pieces of the tally would be matched to verify the amount of the debt. In the case of a king purchasing a wagon, the seller would be the creditor and would be able to pay taxes later by returning the tally stock to the king's exchequer on tax day. Surprisingly, these wooden tally sticks were the basis of medieval Europe's finance – and were used by English kings for the crown's finance through the early nineteenth century.[15]

So wooden sticks are money? Or are they merely recording devices used to measure the king's debt? Or both?

Let's distinguish between money as a liability that is denominated in a money of account, and the technology used to record that liability. We can record a liability through imprints on Mesopotamian clay tablets, notches on sticks, writing in chalk on slate or, later, fountain pen on parchment paper, stamped and milled coins, inked paper notes, and today's electronic entries stored on computer hard drives. These are records of debts, using different technologies.

How the liabilities are recorded is a question of technology. Technology changes over time, often in the never-ending quest to reduce counterfeiting. The *nature* of money does not really change when the recording *technology* changes, although advancing technology might reduce counterfeiting and also make payments easier. It is arguably simpler to pay your bills online than to write and mail checks, or to use "plastic" (credit cards) than to carry cash.[16]

While the march of payments technology will continue – people increasingly use their smartphones for payments, for example – the *nature* of money as the debt of its issuer, denominated in a national money of account (the US dollar, the European Euro, the Chinese RMB) will not change.[17] Admittedly, things are more complex today. Sovereign governments no longer directly spend their coins or tally sticks into existence. All payments from and to government treasuries are now handled by central banks. We'll discuss this in more detail later. This adds a degree of separation between the sovereign and the public that complicates understanding.

As a side note, perhaps the most important original contribution of MMT has been the detailed study of coordination of operations among the treasury, the central bank and private banks that is now required anytime the government spends or collects taxes. The procedures involved can obscure how the government "really spends." While it was obvious two hundred years ago that the national treasury spent by issuing currency, and taxed by receiving its own currency in payment, that is no longer so clear because the central bank stands between the treasury and recipients of government spending as well as between treasury and taxpayers making payments to government.

However, as MMT has shown, nothing of substance has changed. Despite the greater complexity involved, we lose nothing of substance by saying that government spends currency into existence and taxpayers use that currency to pay their obligations to the state. But we will indeed discuss those internal operations in more detail later.

E. The Nature of Money

This has been a rather long excursion into the functions, nature and technology of money, so let us sum up.

1. Money is often defined by its functions: *money is what money does*.
This is not entirely satisfying – sort of like defining a human as an animal that sits on a couch and watches TV while munching chips. We must begin by identifying what functions we think money should perform (medium of exchange, store of value, unit of account, means of payment) and then finding things that perform at least some of those functions. There is a bit of circularity, since if I started from the assumption that money ought to waterski, and then came up with an inventory of things that do waterski, I'd end up with a peculiar list of things that I'd call money. In other words, the choice of "what money does" essentially dictates "what money is" as there must be a correspondence between the two.

2. Even if we do begin by defining money by its functions, what we will find is that those things that function as money have changed significantly over time.
At one time in the not-so-distant past, wooden tally sticks performed many of the functions of money. Today, most money exists only as electronic entries on computerized balance sheets. The "technology" associated with money has changed tremendously.

3. This leads to a different approach. All of those "things" we call money share two characteristics.

The first of these is rather obvious – they are *denominated in a unit of account* that measures their "monetary" value. This unit of account normally varies across nations, with each nation typically choosing its own *money of account* – a topic to which we will return. It is the dollar in the US, the yen in Japan, the pound in the UK, and the RMB in China.

Second, on closer inspection we find that all these money "things" are *records of debts* that are measured in that monetary unit. What we have called *technology* determines how we keep those records – whether it is in the form of notches on sticks, ink on paper, or electronic entries. But we don't want to call all records of debt "money." Not all debts are denominated in money terms. If friends invite you to their home for dinner, you have a social obligation to reciprocate at some point. You do not put a dollar figure on that debt, but you do feel indebted. And we probably do not want to call every monetary debt "money." You may owe $60,000 in student loan debt, and while we would call that a monetary debt, we would not call it *money*.

4. We could think of a *continuum of money debts* – or, better, a three-dimensional money "tetrahedron" with three important characteristics:

(a) *liquidity*
(b) *transferability*
(c) *yield*

These three characteristics are closely linked but can be analyzed separately.

(a) **Liquidity** refers to the ability to convert the asset[18] to cash quickly and with little loss of value. Here we take currency as the referent – it is the most liquid money asset.

A *demand deposit* can be quickly converted to cash with little to no loss of value. That is, you can go to your bank's ATM and immediately withdraw cash from your account, usually without a fee. If, however, you cannot get to your bank, you might be charged a fee at another bank's ATM. Along the liquidity dimension, we would put demand deposits close to cash.

Time deposits, including savings deposits, are somewhat less liquid. Banks can impose wait periods for converting time deposits to demand deposits or cash, and they can charge fees. For example, there is usually a "substantial penalty" for withdrawing funds from a ninety-day certificate of deposit. We place time deposits further out on the liquidity dimension.

Bonds, including government bonds and corporate bonds, are even less liquid. While it is true that one can quickly sell US Treasury or corporate bonds, there can be fees involved and the value of a bond is variable up to its maturity date.[19]

Stocks (equities) can be sold quickly (when the stock market is open), but there can be fees and the value changes from day to day and even minute by minute. Note that unlike bonds, stocks do not commit the issuing firm to pay anything to the holder. These are not monetary debts – IOUs – in the same sense in which bank deposits or corporate bonds are promises to pay. Rather, they are fractional ownership shares in the success or failure of the firm and may earn dividends (a portion of profits). In the event of the shutting down of a firm, shares provide the owner with a claim to residual value, if any remains after paying off higher-order claimants.

Other kinds of assets are typically less liquid: privately owned firms, houses, used cars, collectable art, and productive machinery. Note that these are "real" assets, not "financial" assets; they are not monetary IOUs. They are not "denominated" in money, although they might be sold for money and we might assess a money value for them. Typically, it takes time to sell them and the value is uncertain. We would put them farther out on the liquidity dimension.

(b) **Transferability** refers to ability to pass the monetary debt from hand to hand.

If you write "IOU $5" on a slip of paper, someone who knows you well will probably accept it as a monetary debt. The holder of your IOU will keep it as a record of your debt. When you later present five dollars (say, in cash), you receive back your IOU and tear it up.

While it is unlikely, the original holder could instead pass it along to someone else who also knows you well. This could happen, for example, if the original holder owed that person $5. You would then pay the final holder of your IOU in order to get out of debt. It is not likely that your IOU would pass among very many hands. However, when the government issues a monetary debt in the form of paper money or coins, that IOU is likely to pass through many hands before it finally returns to the government that issued it. By design, cash is highly transferable. When most people think about money, they think first about this characteristic.

A little more than a century ago, banks also typically issued paper notes (most people did not have deposit accounts – those were for richer people), although today in most countries governments have monopolized the issue of paper notes. In the old days, bank notes passed relatively easily from hand to hand, at least in normal times. During financial panics, however, they stopped circulating and a "bank run" might begin in which holders would submit them to the banks that issued them, demanding payment in cash (the government's currency).

Other money debts could also circulate, often if they were "endorsed" by an institution or an individual considered to be highly creditworthy. Historically a variety of kinds of monetary debts circulated after endorsements as "money" that could be used to make payments. For example, merchants used to issue bills of exchange that promised payment at a specific time and location and in a designated currency. Often these were used to finance their purchase of goods that would be sold at medieval "fairs"; they would promise to pay at the fair once the issuer sold the goods at the market.

Sometimes their creditors preferred to sell the bills of exchange to get immediate payment, rather than waiting until the close of the fair. They would sell them at a "discount" (less than the amount promised, which effectively represented an interest payment to the purchaser of the bill). The purchaser might be a bank, which would endorse the bill (adding a signature attesting to a promise that the bill was good) and either make a payment with it or sell it on to another bank (again, at a discount). With a sufficient number of such endorsing signatures, the bill would be said to become "gilt-edged," "as good as gold" (gold coins, that is) as a means of payment.

Because lots of creditworthy endorsers were on the hook, default by the original issuer was unlikely to lead to loss as others had promised to make the debt good – making these gilt-edged debts highly transferable

(c) **Yield** refers to the monetary reward paid on debt. Cash earns no yield – it is said to be "current" (hence, it is called "currency") because there is no term to maturity (it is "instantly" available to be used for purchase or payment of debt).[20] Generally speaking, other financial assets must pay a yield to induce people to hold them. In that sense, yield is a "reward" earned for giving up the "liquidity" of cash. All else equal, the longer the term to maturity, the greater that reward.

The preference for liquidity – what the economist John Maynard Keynes called "liquidity preference" – can vary through time. When optimism reigns in markets, liquidity preference may be low; liquidity preference rises when financial markets' participants begin to worry about their financial positions. This will tend to raise the required "reward" to induce someone to hold less-liquid assets. That is, interest rates will tend to rise to compensate for giving up liquidity. In addition, certainty of payment varies due to the creditworthiness of the issuer. The greater the default risk, the greater the yield required to compensate the holder.

Modern lenders often use "credit scoring" to provide a

measure of the risk of default, charging a higher interest rate the lower the score. Ratings agencies provide a similar service as they rate the creditworthiness of governments, firms, and securitized loans (such as mortgages); these ratings go into determining the yield earned on the monetary debts. Modern credit instruments can be exceedingly complex, making calculation of the yield difficult. Still, for our purposes, it is sufficient to understand that those monetary debts thought to be safest and most liquid will offer the lowest yields. This is why cash pays zip and sovereign government debt usually pays the lowest interest rates in the government's own currency (given maturity – all else equal, a thirty-year government bond will tend to pay a higher rate than a two-year bond due to the longer maturity[21]).

F. Conclusion

So . . . what is money? First and foremost it is the unit of account in which we measure nominal value. Like all units of measurement, the money of account needs to be socially sanctioned – whether the "foot" or the "meter," the "gallon" or the "liter," or the "solar month" or the "lunar month." In almost all cases, the money of account is chosen by governments and typically each nation has its own. We call it the dollar in the US.

Throughout history, we have used a variety of methods of keeping track of money amounts. We have kept records on clay tablets, on notched wooden sticks, on stamped metal coins, on various kinds of paper, and increasingly in electronic form on computer hard drives. Among the most important records in money terms are the records of money debts and credits – I Owe You's and You Owe Me's. Most of those records of debts are kept locked away in safety until Redemption Day, when they can be burned. However, some kinds of records of debts can be used in payments, passing from hand to hand among "third parties" that played no role in the original recording of the debt. Some of these records can be held as a store of money value by third parties. And some can be used in payment of debts by third parties to other third parties. We have discussed a hierarchy of money liabilities, as well as the main characteristics that determine general acceptability of such IOUs: liquidity, transferability, and yield.

You've got your choice: just how liquid do you want your portfolio to be? Or to look at it the other way round: how much do we have to pay you to give up liquidity? The interest you earn holding a less liquid asset is your reward for giving up liquidity. That was Keynes's meaning when he used the phrase "liquidity preference." You want maximum liquidity? Then hold cash – the government's IOU. Are you willing to give up some liquidity in order to earn some interest? Then hold a certificate of deposit at an insured bank – you can get the cash in ninety days, or even earlier, but you'll pay a "substantial penalty for early withdrawal." If you are even more patient, you can probably get a higher return for holding a ten-year US Treasury bond.

Note that none of those things we just listed has any risk of default – the bank liability is insured by the FDIC (Federal Deposit Insurance Corporation) and the US government will not default on cash or bonds. If you are willing to incur some risk of default, you can hold uninsured liabilities of financial institutions or corporate bonds. They will pay you more interest for incurring that risk. They might also be less liquid – so you can earn the liquidity premium, too. Hey, if you want even more risk and even less liquidity, accept an IOU from a complete stranger!

Maybe we want to reserve the word "money" for highly liquid IOUs that don't carry default risk. For many purposes, that makes sense. While "anyone can create money" – that is, write "IOU five bucks" – such debts are not equal in the eyes of the beholder. It is sensible to limit the term to government's currency (cash and central bank reserves), insured bank liabilities (checking and saving deposits), and

perhaps some other very liquid, safe, and short-term liabilities issued by governments and financial institutions.
Those working in financial markets often colloquially call
these "cash assets." We need to keep in mind that precisely
where we draw the line is somewhat arbitrary.

In the next chapter we will examine in more detail how
those most acceptable IOUs make their way into the economy. We focus in particular on the liabilities issued by
government and by the special financial institutions that
we call banks. While "anyone can issue money," not all
money is created equal. It is important to explore how the
most privileged money IOUs are issued.

2

Where Does Money Come From?

Now that we understand what money is, in this chapter we examine where money comes from. We start with a simplified explanation of how money gets into the economy. In the first section we will look at the state's money, including the roles played by the treasury and the central bank, and then turn to private creation of money by private banks, supported by the central bank. We finish with a somewhat more detailed explanation of how the treasury, the central bank, and private banks cooperate to issue government money as well as government bonds.

A. Money Creation Simplified: The State's Money

As discussed in the introduction and chapter 1, we should not think of money as an invention of the private sector. Money is and always has been a "state money" – a creation of the authorities who choose a money of account and impose obligations to "drive" the currency.

Privately issued debts are denominated in a state money of account. As my professor, Hyman Minsky, used to say,

"Everyone can create money" – that is, issue a liability denominated in the money of account – but "the problem is to get it accepted." We'll come back to that.

But let's begin at the beginning: the state's own money.

As we already learned, when you hold the government's currency, you are a creditor and the government is the debtor. You can use the government's currency to pay down your own debts, including your tax obligations. When you use currency to pay taxes, both you and the government are simultaneously redeemed: you no longer owe taxes, and the government is no longer your debtor.

As discussed, in the old days government simply imposed obligations (such as taxes) and spent its own liabilities that would be accepted in payment. It could stamp coins, cut tally sticks, or print paper notes to spend as currency. These would be denominated in the government's own money of account. Government would then accept this currency back in payment. What did the government do with the tax revenue? Burned it or shredded it or melted it for re-coining.

Until a few centuries ago, the obligations imposed on the government's subjects (monarchies) or citizens (democracies) usually took the form of tithes, tribute, fines, and fees; however, taxes gradually became more important from the eighteenth century. As these obligations had to be paid in the currency, they drove a demand for it. Spending by government must come before taxes can be paid in currency – until the government spends some currency, no one can pay taxes using that currency. We also noted that the government cannot run out of its own currency. It can always print, notch, or stamp more paper notes, tally sticks, or metal coins.

Today it is a bit more complicated. We'll need to dig into the details a bit to see how modern governments spend, using their central banks. Indeed, there are "two degrees of separation" between the government and its citizens so far as spending and taxes are concerned. This somewhat veils the processes and makes it easy to reach the wrong conclusions. Most people, including most economists, are "dazed and confused" about all this. We need to lift the veil of fog.

B. How the Central Bank Creates "Money"

Modern government spending involves two entities – the central bank and the treasury – and their activities are necessarily coordinated. The central bank is responsible for monetary policy (as everyone knows) but it is also the government's bank (which most people forget). The treasury is the entity charged with spending and taxing for the government, but it actually makes all payments (and receives all tax payments) through the central bank.

While many economists draw a sharp dividing line between monetary and fiscal policy, it is impossible to maintain such a division in the real world because there are monetary impacts of fiscal policy – money is always involved in fiscal policy actions (that is, spending and taxing). Still it is useful to think of a division of responsibilities when it comes to the creation of government money. To put it simply, the central bank lends government money into existence while the treasury spends it into existence.

Remember it this way: *the central bank lends, the treasury spends.*

That should not be too surprising. After all, the central bank is a bank. Bank lending creates money – as we will explain in more detail later. This is true also for the central bank. The main difference is this: private banks today create deposits as their "money"; the central bank creates bank reserves plus central bank notes as its money.

When the central bank lends, it directly creates reserves – that is the form its lending takes. The central bank lends reserves to private banks by crediting their reserve accounts at the central bank. This is simply a keystroke credit to the borrowing bank's balance sheet. The private bank's reserve account is much like your deposit account at your bank – sort of a checking account. Private banks make payments to each other using this "checking account," just as you write checks on your bank account to make payments.

Reserves are liabilities of the central bank, and assets of the bank that got the credit. The central bank holds the private bank's IOU, on which the private bank pays interest to the central bank. Central banks do not normally lend directly to other kinds of firms or to households – although if it allowed them to have "checking accounts" (at the central bank), this would be easy enough to do by simply crediting the checking account.

Finally, central banks also create reserves when they buy assets. Typically, central banks buy government bonds and sometimes also private bonds (such as mortgage-backed securities) from private banks. When they do so, they credit the reserve account of the selling bank. This is called an "open market purchase." Central banks can also sell bonds to a private bank, debiting the bank's reserves – called an "open market sale." So central bank purchases are used to increase reserves held by banks, and sales are used to reduce reserves. Keep that in mind. This is a large part of what is normally called "monetary policy." Note this is a minor exception to our rule that *central banks lend and treasuries spend*. Central banks do buy a limited range of *financial* assets – but these purchases are undertaken to implement monetary policy, not to move resources to the government sector, which is what fiscal policy is largely about.

Reserves can always be converted on demand to central bank notes (our green paper dollars in the US). That conversion is done by the central bank to meet the demand of the public for cash. Every time you go to an ATM machine to withdraw cash, your bank must convert its reserve deposits at the central bank to cash. Private banks cannot print up cash, but rather must order it from the central bank – and they "pay for" the cash through a debit to their reserves. Modern central banks *never* refuse to provide the cash the public demands. Even if banks are short reserves to make the conversion, the central bank will lend reserves to them so that they can convert them to the cash the public demands.

C. How Modern Treasuries Spend through their Central Banks

In chapter 1 we discussed sovereign money creation that more or less accurately captured the essence of sovereign spending in the era before central banks were created – that is to say, the way things worked for the first 4,000–6,000 years since money originated. The treasury simply spent its own currency to make payments, and collected its own currency as tax receipts. We rarely do it that way anymore. The modern treasury uses its bank, the central bank, to make and receive payments on its behalf. (That isn't so strange – firms and households make and receive payments through their private banks.)

So let us now move on to a more realistic explanation of the way things work today. Here we will separate the treasury and central bank. The treasury is tasked with implementing the budget approved by elected representatives and with collecting the taxes imposed by congress or parliament. But it is the central bank that makes and receives payments for the treasury. The treasury holds a deposit account at the central bank that is debited when payments are made by the central bank and credited when payments are received by the central bank.

We will begin our discussion by including a private bank with an account at the central bank. We also include two other private entities – a taxpayer who owes taxes and a contractor who performs services for the government. For simplicity we assume they both use the same bank, although nothing of significance changes if one of them were to use another bank. (See section F below for payments between banks.) When the treasury spends, it issues a check to the contractor for services. The contractor presents that to the bank, which credits the contractor's deposit account. The bank sends the check to the central bank, which credits its reserves. The central bank will post a debit to the treasury's account to balance the credit to reserves.

Note that there are two financial impacts on the private sector: the contractor's deposit account rises by the amount of the treasury's spending, and the bank's reserves also rise by the same amount. There is one "real" impact – the contractor sold a resource (say, a new window for a government building) to the government equal in value to the deposit received. In other words, the result of these financial transactions was to move a real resource to the public sector.

From the point of view of the government, that is the purpose of this part of the monetary system – to obtain real resources for government use. From the point of view of the contractor, the financial transactions "monetized" the service provided – enabling the contractor to sell a product in exchange for a demand deposit credit. In terms of balance sheet impacts, the contractor's asset (the window sold) is debited and the contractor's demand deposit (asset) is credited. The bank's liabilities go up by the amount of the demand deposit owed to the contractor, but the bank's assets go up by the amount of its reserve credit at the central bank.

Finally, we need to understand the internal accounting between the treasury and the central bank. When the treasury spends, the central bank credits a private bank's reserves and debits the treasury's deposit at the central bank. When taxes are paid, the central bank debits a private bank's reserves and credits the treasury's deposit account at the central bank. These internal accounting procedures are invisible to the nongovernment sector – which sees only the impacts on private bank deposits and reserves, as well as the sale of output to the government. The internal accounting has no impact on the rest of the economy.

It is sort of like the internal accounting of a household: a spouse could promise to pay the other spouse $10 for washing the dishes; or the parents could promise a weekly allowance to the kids. All of this can be kept track of in an accounts book, with net settlements at the end of the year. No one outside the family would know, or care, what was going on inside the household's internal accounts. All that would matter is the external accounting: did the household make the car and mortgage payments, receive wages for outside work, and pay taxes to the government? Who owed whom within the household would be of no concern – at least until the spouses go to divorce court!

The US Treasury and the Fed do keep internal accounts and they make sure the accounts balance. They've adopted procedures to ensure that the Treasury always has a positive balance in its account that can be debited whenever the Fed makes a payment on behalf of the Treasury. These involve private banks and bond markets, too. The procedures are complicated but foolproof. How do we know? Because Treasury checks are never bounced by the Fed due to insufficient funds. Even though there are hundreds of millions of dollars paid and received daily, and even if the Treasury spends trillions more dollars than it receives in taxes over the course of a year, no Treasury check gets bounced. That's pretty good evidence that the Fed and Treasury know what they are doing.

But in any case, those internal accounts are of no consequence to anyone outside the government sector (treasury and central bank). All that matters is that treasury spending leads to reserve credits to private banks, and tax payments lead to reserve debits.

We'll dig a little deeper in the next sections.

D. How Are Taxes Paid?

When the taxpayer pays taxes, the financial transactions are the reverse of the process of government spending: the taxpayer writes a check on a bank deposit that is received by the treasury. The treasury sends it to the central bank that debits reserves and credits the treasury's deposit account at the central bank. The bank debits the taxpayer's deposit account. The net result of the tax payment is that the taxpayer's deposits have been reduced and the bank's reserves have declined; additionally, the treasury's deposit at its central bank has risen and the taxpayer's tax liability owed to the treasury has been reduced.

Note that it is the treasury's spending that moves the real resource to the public sector, not the tax payment. Paying taxes is just a financial transaction – a debit of the bank's reserves – although it is the need to pay taxes that drives the public's desire to obtain currency that can be used in "redemption" (paying taxes to eliminate tax debt).

Recall that reserves are the government's liability; more specifically, reserves are the central bank's debt. Just as payment of taxes in our simplest model above returns currency to the government, payment of taxes in this more realistic model "returns" reserves to the government. The reserves are stricken from the private bank's deposit at the central bank.

We still use the term "tax return" in reference to paying taxes – indeed, our term "revenue" derives from the word for "return." What returns when taxes are paid? The government's own liability that it had spent into existence. Government doesn't really spend tax revenue. Even today, the government does not spend what is "returned."

While it is a common misperception that government "spends taxes," that is not really possible. When you pay your taxes, your deposit is simply debited. Where did the money go? It was stricken from your account. There's nothing that the government can spend. When the government spends, it takes the form of a credit to your bank's reserves, and your bank credits your private bank account. The Treasury did not "spend" the tax; rather, the Fed made a payment on the Treasury's behalf by crediting a bank's reserves. The Fed does not need "tax revenue" in order to make that payment – it simply keystrokes a credit to a reserve account.

When the colonial American governments received paper notes in payment, they burned them. When the king received back tally sticks, his exchequer matched and burned them. Today, payment of taxes leads to a debit of a taxpayer's demand deposits and a debit of a private bank's reserves. Our government can't really spend either of these. Nor are these required before the government spends – which takes the form of keystroke credits.

We have learned that banks use reserves when making payments to the treasury. This occurs when their customers pay taxes by writing checks against deposit accounts. The taxpayer's bank must make a payment of reserves equal to the tax payment. While it appears to the taxpayer that her deposits at a private bank are used to pay the taxes, actually the tax payment is made through a deduction of the reserves of the taxpayer's bank.

This is not semantics. It is accounting. The taxpayer's deposit account is debited – to be sure – but the taxes are paid for her by her bank in the form of the government's own liability, central bank reserves. Taxes have always been paid this way – by submitting back to the government its own liability. Where do these reserves come from? Well, they had to come from the central bank – that is the only source of reserves since these are the liabilities of the central bank.

What if the private bank has no reserves to debit when a taxpayer pays taxes? There are several possibilities: the central bank will lend the reserves needed. Or other private banks with more reserves than they need can lend them to the bank that requires them (in the US, this is done in what is called the Fed Funds market). Or the bank can sell assets to obtain reserves – usually the bank will sell treasury bonds. If the bank sells the bonds to another private bank, the buying bank will use reserves – and the central bank will debit the reserves of the buying bank and credit the reserves of the selling bank so that it can use these when the taxpayer pays taxes.

Finally, as discussed in section B above, banks that need reserves can also sell bonds to the central bank. In this case the central bank creates reserves and credits them to the selling bank. The private bank exchanges a government bond for reserves, and then uses reserves to make the payment of taxes for the customer. (In practice, the timing does not have to be precise: the central bank allows time for a bank to acquire the reserves needed to cover a tax payment, essentially allowing an overdraft – called "float" – until the reserves are obtained. In the real world, banks are making and receiving thousands – even millions – of payments a day, so the central bank simply clears payments and settles up later.)

The key takeaway from all this is that for taxes to be paid, banks must have reserves that can be debited – so that the "return" of a government liability can be completed. There are three ways, and only three ways, that reserves can get into the banks: treasury spending, central bank lending, or central bank purchases of assets. In other words, the reserves must come from the government (treasury plus central bank) before taxes can be paid. Just as in the old days, when currency had to be spent before taxes could be paid, reserves have to be created by government before taxes can be paid.

We have also seen that when bank reserves are debited through a tax payment, the treasury's deposit account at the central bank is credited. And, as we noted, when the treasury spends, the central bank debits its deposit account and credits the reserves of the bank(s) that receive payments from the treasury. Many erroneously jump to the conclusion that taxes must be paid first in order to get positive balances in the treasury's account at the central bank. However, reserves must get into the banking system before taxes are paid. Furthermore, there are other ways to get positive credits in the treasury's account – let's see in the next section.

E. Do Treasury Checks Bounce due to Insufficient Funds?

Real-world procedures can get complex and timing can complicate issues. One must remember that on any given day the treasury receives hundreds of thousands or even millions of tax payments and makes as many payments. It is impossible to predict how much will be received in taxes, and how many treasury checks will be presented for payment, on any day. In the USA, the Fed and Treasury communicate each morning to make projections for the day's payments, receipts, and net balances. However, those projections will (inevitably) be off to varying degrees.

How does the treasury deal with errors? Well, one way is to keep a positive balance in its account (just as you do); however, in practice that balance is usually quite small. Tax receipts tend to come in bunches (on tax days!) while payments are more evenly spread through the year (although concentrated around the beginning of each month). And if the treasury is annually spending more than it is receiving in taxes (as almost all treasuries do!), it will consistently find itself short. So "errors" are commonplace. What happens if the treasury writes a check in an amount greater than its deposit at its central bank? Would the central bank "bounce" the check for insufficient funds?

The short answer is "no." Bouncing a treasury check would lead to big political and economic problems. Imagine retirees living on social security whose monthly checks begin bouncing because the treasury's funds are "insufficient." Imagine what would happen when financial markets got wind of the bouncing checks. The entire modern financial system is built on the belief that government liabilities are good assets, that government pays its debts when they come due, and that holding a government check or other government debt is "good money."

And, in fact, it doesn't happen – treasury checks are not bounced by central banks. While central banks – including the Fed – do not want to publicly announce that they offer overdraft facilities (essentially increasing treasury deposits whenever necessary to prevent checks from bouncing), we have three reasons to believe that they do so routinely.

1. *Sheer volume of daily clearing.* In the US, the federal government spends on average about $13 million per minute (growing each year); tax revenue varies considerably depending on the state of the economy, but since spending over the year almost always exceeds taxes collected, let us assume tax revenues average about $10 million a minute.[1] However, the timing of these money streams is very different. Spending rises sharply around the first of the month – when social security, various kinds of welfare, and retirement payments go out and deposit accounts of recipients are credited. Tax receipts are bunched around quarterly due dates as well as in the weeks before April 15 (the usual federal income tax deadline). Traditionally, the Treasury has aimed to maintain a balance of $5 billion in its deposit account at the Fed at the end of each day.[2] That provides a bit of a cushion, but not much given that its daily spending averages about $10 billion. Over the course of the day, the mismatch between the flows of spending and tax revenue could wipe out the cushion. For this reason, the central bank provides "daylight" overdrafts – just as your private bank might do for you if you have opted for overdraft protection.

2. *Consequences of bouncing.* The consequences of bouncing treasury checks could shake confidence in the payments system itself. This is why the central banks lend reserves so that private banks can clear payments. Modern central banks have a laser-like focus on the payments system, going to extraordinary measures – if necessary – to make sure checks clear at "par." That is, a check drawn against the Bank of Anaheim that is written for $100 will be accepted at the Bank of Buffalo at a value of $100. And a US Treasury check written

for $100 will be accepted at every bank in America at a value of $100.

3. *The Fed's operational manual.* In the Q&A section of the operational manual used by the Fed's staff the question is posed: what do we do if we receive a Treasury check but the Treasury's deposit has already dropped to zero? Answer: clear the check and enter a negative number. That is an overdraft.

We have stated that the government usually runs a budget deficit and earlier we have argued that this is not a cause for concern because the government is not like a household. However, if – as we just presumed – government spends $13 million a minute but tax revenue is only $10 million a minute, what are the consequences for the accounting between the treasury and the central bank? Yes, the very short-run implication could be an overdraft, but what if this happens day after day after day? At that pace, it would accumulate to almost $1.6 trillion in overdrafts over the course of the year.

The easiest solution would be for the central bank to just lend deposits to the treasury. The balancing item for the central bank would be the treasury's IOU. If deficits continued, the treasury's debt to the central bank would grow at the same pace as the lending. Could this go on forever? Yes, indeed. The central bank cannot run out of deposits to lend to the treasury, and the treasury can just keep writing IOUs to the central bank. But most rich countries have imposed rules that prevent this sort of thing except in emergencies.

For example, a common rule is that the central bank cannot provide overnight "overdrafts" to the treasury – the treasury must have "money in its account" to clear checks. While you can negotiate an overdraft facility with your private bank, the US Treasury cannot have one with the Fed (at least on an overnight basis).

Second, central banks often are prohibited from buying treasury bonds directly from the treasury (the "new issue" market), but instead must buy them from anyone else (the "secondary" market). It is a strange prohibition if you think about it. It is somewhat like telling you that you can get a mortgage loan or a car loan from any bank except your own bank. But the thinking is that this forces the treasury to sell bonds to "markets," which is supposed to force "market discipline" on the government.

To comply with these rules, the central bank and Treasury in the US have developed procedures to ensure there are always "funds in the account." These procedures include creation of relations with special banks that receive payments for the Treasury and special dealer banks that stand ready to always purchase Treasury securities. When the Treasury expects to be "short," it moves funds from these special banks to the central bank and sells securities to special dealer banks to replenish demand deposits in those special banks.

The central bank also cooperates by ensuring these private banks have access to reserves that are needed to shift deposits or to buy Treasury securities. If necessary, the central bank lends reserves (or allows "float," which is a type of overdraft, as we have seen). And if the banks decide they do not want to hold Treasury securities, they sell them on to the central bank that stands ready to buy them in the "open market." This effectively undermines the prohibition that prevents the Treasury from selling securities to the central bank, since they are sold round about through the banks and hence on to the central bank. There is no prohibition on central bank purchases of government bonds in the secondary markets.[3]

What many people forget is that the central bank has two overriding concerns. First, it needs the payments system to operate smoothly – and that means that it does not want checks to bounce. Above all, the government's own checks must clear. Second, it wants to hit its overnight interest rate target (Fed Funds rate, or bank rate). That means it must accommodate bank demand for reserves – including reserves that banks need to cover Treasury operations (transfers from tax and loan accounts, and purchases of Treasury securities). We will examine interest rate setting later, but all modern central banks operate with an overnight interest rate target – and would have difficulty hitting it if banks were short reserves. (Shortages of reserves would cause the overnight interest rate to rise above the central bank's target.)

All of this gets technical but the "proof of the pudding" that the central bank and treasury know what they are doing "is in the eating" – so to speak. In spite of the complexity, Treasury checks do not bounce, and the central bank does hit its interest rate target (within a margin of error that is discretionary). Even in the case of Japan – which has an outstanding government debt-to-GDP ratio of more than 2.5 to 1 (that is, the government debt-to-GDP ratio is 250 percent), and the biggest sustained budget deficits the world has ever seen – the operations run smoothly, with treasury checks clearing and the Bank of Japan keeping overnight rates essentially at zero.

So, when we hear politicians proclaiming "the government has run out of money," as President Obama did on many occasions, we can be sure that they are wrong. Sovereign government cannot run out of its own keystrokes.

We now turn to the "private" part of the monetary system. In the final section we re-examine government creation of currency, bringing in the central bank as well as relations with private banks. As we'll see, it is not as simple as the system we've described so far. But the conclusions still hold.

F. How Banks Create Money

In modern economies, banks play a special role. They are typically chartered by the government – to undertake specific sanctioned activities, one must have a charter. (To be sure, the lines between banks and "shadow banks" have become increasingly blurred over the past three or four decades.) Banks are normally subject to special rules and oversight by government authorities. They also have special access to lending by the central bank. And in most countries a large portion of their liabilities is government-insured.

What that means is that bank liabilities are special – they are liquid (as defined in chapter 1) and there is no default risk on government-insured deposits. This helps to make bank deposits widely accepted as safe assets to hold. At the same time, banks benefit from these government "back-stops" (lending by the central bank and insurance from the treasury). Banks can issue liabilities that pay lower interest rates because they are deemed to be safer.

There may also be (perhaps unintentional) benefits to the biggest banks that are considered to be "too big to fail." The perception that government will always rescue a big bank will allow it to issue even uninsured liabilities at low interest rates. People figure that no matter what the bank does, government will bail it, and them, out. Further, a bank's stock prices will tend to be higher if investors believe there is little chance government will allow it to fail. And it might be able to get away with riskier behavior (such as running lower capital ratios and buying riskier assets) if it is thought to be "too big to fail." In turn, banks that are too big to fail may be able to offer loans at lower interest rates (since their costs can be lower) – giving them an advantage over other lenders.

These are issues of concern to bank regulators and we will not pursue them in detail, but in the next chapter will discuss the possibility that too much lending (especially risky lending) could lead to financial crises. For all these reasons, banks play a special role in the financial system, and the biggest banks may be deemed to be even more special than the small ones. This is why government pays special attention to them – protecting and regulating them.

As we will explain in detail, private bank deposits are created (mostly) when banks make loans. Private banks use their reserve accounts at the central bank when they need to clear checks (that is, make payments to one another).

Bank reserves, in turn, are created by central bank loans to the private banks. Both "private money" in the form of bank deposits and "government money" in the form of reserves are created by keystrokes – something we cannot run out of.

Historically, what are called "commercial banks" (those that specialize in making short-term loans and issuing demand deposits) have been the major lenders to private business (especially to smaller and medium-sized firms) to finance the production process. They have also been the major players in what we call the "payments system" as their deposits were used to make most payments. Indeed, the loan-making activities and the deposit-provision services have been closely linked. Let's explore that relationship.

As we have previously mentioned, deposits are created when banks make loans. If commercial banks make loans to finance production, they are creating the deposits that are used to hire labor and other resources used in the production process. Those deposits then "circulate" the output that is produced – providing the means of payment used by households to buy the output from firms that paid their wages to produce the output. Incomes generated by production are received in the form of commercial bank deposits and these then can be used to buy the consumer goods produced. We will use this view of the relation between commercial banking and production to trace the creation of private money through the loan-making process.

Of course, the real world has always been more complicated, and complexity has increased greatly over the past few decades due to tremendous financial innovation. The biggest commercial banks have moved away from the traditional lending business, and much of the payments system now takes place outside the commercial banks. The lines between commercial banks and investment banks (that traditionally financed investment projects undertaken by firms) are no longer clear-cut. And the rise of a wide variety of types of financial activities that are referred to with the rather all-encompassing term *shadow banking* has further complicated matters.

Still, our understanding of money creation can be improved by studying the process through which traditional commercial banking financed production. And the majority of banks (in terms of number – at least in the US where we still have thousands of small banks) still behave this way, even though the behemoths (that account for most of the volume of assets held by banks) do not.

So how do banks create money?

We now turn to an examination of money creation by private financial institutions. We do not need to imagine money as manna from heaven, but rather see it as the creation of purchasing power controlled by the banker. We will begin with a simple description of the money creation process, and will gradually introduce more complexity.

Models are often used by economists to simplify exposition. By stripping away details we can focus on the most important processes. Unfortunately, if too many details are removed, a model can be misleading. For example, a lot of conventional economic models leave money out of the analysis entirely, modeling simple economies that function without money. When money is then added later, it plays no important role. We are not going to do that, however.

We will begin our model by assuming that money is important; indeed, the production process itself must begin with money. A firm that wishes to engage in production must first obtain money in order to purchase inputs (labor, intermediate goods, and raw materials) to the production process. Further, we will assume that the firm engages in production in order to sell the output for money. The hope, of course, is to make profits – which requires that the goods or services are sold for *more* money than the firm had to spend on the inputs. All of this probably sounds obvious to you as it captures features of the real world. However – believe it or not – most models used by economists do not begin and end with money.

For the purposes of our model we also want to avoid any "infinite regress" problems. It would be easy enough to presume that the firm begins the production process with money it has saved from previous sales of output. The problem with starting there is that we have not explained how the firm had financed the production of the output that it already sold for money. If we were simply to assert that the previous production was financed by sales that occurred even earlier, we've got a "chicken and egg" problem: where did money come from in the first place?

Hence, we will begin our model with a firm that wishes to produce output, but has no hoarded money to purchase inputs to production. This allows us to examine how money gets created in the first place: the firm will approach a banker for a loan.

Note also that we do not want to rely on an infinite regress argument regarding the loan. It is frequently assumed that the banker takes in deposits and then lends them out. That creates another "chicken and egg" problem: where did the deposit come from? One response could be that someone deposits a check or cash into the deposit account, but that just raises another question about the origins of the check or cash that was deposited. So, if we are to begin at the beginning, we must start from the creation of money.

Following from the discussion in chapter 1, we know that "money" is simply a record of a debt. Bank deposits are the liabilities of banks and are created when they make loans. Really all that the bank needs to do is to credit the deposit account of the borrower. In the case we will examine, the producing firm is the borrower and the money it needs to begin the production process is created by its bank. The bank will hold the loan (the "note," which is the liability of the firm) as its asset, while it credits the demand deposit of the firm.

The producer wanting to hire labor and to purchase resources needed for the production process submits a *prospectus* to the banker. While the banker looks at past performance as well as wealth pledged as collateral, most important is the likelihood that the producer's prospects are good. Assessing creditworthiness is called "underwriting." If the banker believes the producer will be able to make payments on the loan, a loan is advanced. In the old days, the bank would actually print bank notes to lend; today the bank simply credits the deposit of the firm. (In return, the firm signs the loan document – the "note" held by the bank – promising to make interest and principal payments to the bank.) The firm will use its created deposit to purchase inputs to the production process.

Since we want to focus on bank creation of money, for our simplest model, assume there is no cash – all payments are made using the bank's deposit accounts. Households supply labor and other resources used by the firm, and they purchase the firm's output as consumers. They receive and use "bank money" – deposits of their wages – to make such purchases.

For our simplest model, we will assume that there is only one bank, one household, and one firm. The firm hires labor and purchases raw materials in order to produce output. Payments are made by writing checks on the deposit account at the bank. The recipient of the firm's spending deposits the checks at the bank, resulting in credits to the household's own deposit account and debits to the firm's account. (Note that all these transactions can be done "electronically" on the balance sheet of the bank – there is no need for physical checks.) Once the firm has finished producing goods or services for sale, they are sold to households. This reverses the transactions – the household writes a check on its deposit account and the firm deposits this in favor of its own account. The bank debits the household's deposit and credits the firm's deposit.

In the final step, the firm repays its original loan by writing a check on its deposit account. The bank debits the firm's account and returns the firm's "note." The loan is repaid, and the firm can burn or shred the evidence of its IOU. Note that when the loan is repaid, the bank's deposits are struck from the bank's balance sheet, too. (Both the firm and the bank are simultaneously "redeemed" – as discussed earlier.)

Obviously, we have presented a very simple model of the loan- and deposit-creation process: we assumed only one firm, one household, and one bank. The firm and the household used the same bank. The firm's spending on labor and raw materials (purchased from the household) equaled the household's spending on the firm's output (meaning the firm earned no profits and the household did not save). The firm was able to repay to the bank exactly the amount it had borrowed (so the bank earned no interest).[4]

A more realistic model would need to take account of numerous complications (including profits, saving, interest, cash withdrawals, bank reserves, intermediate products produced by other firms, and bank capital), but even this example shows loan- and deposit-creating procedures, and highlights what happens when payments are made using bank deposits. However, because we actually live in a world with many banks, households, and firms, payments typically involve at least two banks. Banks clear accounts with one another by cancelling ("netting") claims against one another or by using deposits in correspondent banks.[5] Net clearing among banks is usually done on the central bank's balance sheet.

We will expand our model to include two banks. We will assume that the banks have *reserve* accounts at the central bank that they use to make payments to each other for clearing.

Reserve accounts are like checking accounts held at the central bank. Assume the firm uses Bank 1, while the household uses Bank 2. When the firm writes a check on Bank 1 to make a payment to the household, the check is deposited in Bank 2. Bank 2 presents the check to Bank 1 for "clearing." The central bank debits the reserves of Bank 1 and credits reserves of Bank 2. When the household then writes a check on Bank 2 to make a payment to the firm, the process is reversed: Bank 1 presents that check to Bank 2 for clearing. The central bank credits the reserves of Bank 1 and debits the reserves of Bank 2.

How do banks get reserves in the first place? Remember that reserves are simply deposits created by the central bank. Just as a private bank creates deposits (in favor of the borrower) when it makes a loan, the central bank creates reserves (in favor of the borrowing bank) when it makes a loan. (As mentioned above, central banks also create reserves when they purchase assets, such as government bonds.) So the central bank can simply credit the reserves of a borrowing bank, holding the bank's IOU.

The central bank generally charges a low interest rate (called the "discount rate" in the US) for such loans. Central banks routinely lend reserves as banks need them for clearing to make sure that the payments system functions smoothly. Otherwise, bank checks would not clear in a timely fashion – which at the extreme would endanger what is called "par clearing." This is the acceptance by one bank of a check drawn on another bank "at par," or "dollar for dollar," as we saw earlier.

Today most payments are made electronically, taking the form of electronic credits and debits to accounts. You can access your bank account via the internet and instruct your bank to debit your account to make a payment to your utility company. Since your utility company probably uses a different bank, your bank will need to make the payment for you by instructing the central bank (the Fed in the USA) to debit its account and credit the account of the utility company's bank.

Technological change has shortened the time required for such transactions and central banks are keenly focused on making sure the payments system functions smoothly and quickly. Like any banker, the Fed or the Bank of England or any central bank of any country "keystrokes" money into existence. Central bank money takes the form of reserves (or paper notes[6]), created to make payments for customers (banks or the national treasury) or to make purchases for its own account (treasury securities or mortgage-backed securities, for example). A central bank cannot run out of keystrokes.

To conclude our inquiry so far: *where does money come from?*

When you go to a ball game – let us say to Fenway Park to watch Boston play Tampa Bay (baseball teams) – and five runs are scored in the sixth inning, do you wonder where the scorekeeper got those five runs to post up? Does the scorekeeper[7] have to borrow them from somebody? Or "tax" them away from Boston to award to Tampa Bay? Of course not.

In the old days, the scorekeeper would have to sort through a stack of numbered cards to find one reading "5" to pin to the scoreboard. If she or he ran out, she or he might have to take out a large marker pen and create a new one. Today, the scorekeeper just uses a finger to strike the number 5 on a keyboard. She or he cannot run out. Where do the runs come from? *Keystrokes.* What do they represent? *Scorekeeping. Tallying. Accounting.* Today's banks operate in the same manner. Where do the deposits come from? Keystrokes. Scorekeeping. Tallying. Accounting.

If you receive a wage payment from your employer, the bank keystrokes a positive entry to your deposits; at the same time, your employer's deposits are marked down by the same amount. Where do banks get those deposits to credit to your account? Keystrokes. And where do the deposits debited from your employer's account go? Keystroked away. Where does a bank get the $180,000 it lends to you to buy a house? Where does the central bank get the reserves it lends to private banks? Keystrokes.

It makes no more sense to worry about those questions that it does to worry about where the scorekeeper found the five runs to credit to Tampa Bay in the sixth inning. In baseball we call it scorekeeping. Banks also keep score but we call that *accounting* – and the accounting is in money, not runs.

G. Why Does Government Sell Bonds?

If government can simply keystroke to make payments, why does it sell bonds? Does it really need to borrow its own money? Wouldn't it be a disaster if the "bond vigilantes" went on strike and refused to lend to finance government's spending? The short answer is "No" – bonds sales are not really a borrowing operation. And if the vigilantes refused to buy the bonds (an unlikely scenario), that would not prevent the government from spending.

Let's examine an alternative view of bond sales, developed by a hedge fund manager named Warren Mosler (who played a key role in the creation of MMT). He used to specialize in trading in sovereign government bond markets. Back before the creation of the Euro, in the early 1990s, everyone was worried about Italian budget deficits and debt – the government's deficit was 10 percent of GDP, its debt ratio was over 100 percent of GDP, and many were expecting default. As a result, Italian government bonds were falling in price (interest rates were rising) and Warren saw a possible profit opportunity.

He was thinking about central bank open market operations. When the central bank sells treasury bonds, that is called a monetary policy operation. When the treasury sells bonds, it is called a fiscal borrowing operation.

But Warren knew that the functional impact is precisely the same: banks exchange reserves to buy government bonds. He realized that the function of bond sales – whether new issues by the treasury or open market sales by the central bank – is to drain reserves from banks. As such, it is a monetary policy operation, not a borrowing operation. Indeed, banks have to have the reserves before they can pay for the bonds – whether sold by the treasury or by the central bank – because they pay for the bonds using their reserves at the central bank. So government must issue the reserves *before* it sells bonds. And if it can issue the reserves before it "borrows" them (sells bonds) then it doesn't need to borrow at all!

Well, Warren thought, if bonds are not a borrowing operation, and if governments cannot run out of their own money, then Italy is not in danger of defaulting! Warren flew over to Italy and explained this to the Italian treasury. And then he bought up their outstanding bonds at a cheap price. And of course Italy never defaulted and Warren profited as Italian government bond prices recovered. He's now the father of several rival populist MMT groups in Italy. (It is almost like the rivalry among the Judean People's Front, the Popular Front of Judea, and the People's Front of Judea in Monty Python's *The Life of Brian* – if you know that movie.) He fills *futbol* (soccer) stadiums when he goes there to speak about MMT.

Most people think Uncle Sam has to borrow to pay for spending – and point to government bonds as evidence that Uncle Sam has borrowed $28 trillion (as of 2021). But that would be like you borrowing your own IOUs: Uncle Sam doesn't borrow dollars, he creates them in the form of Fed reserves when he spends. Reserves are effectively deposits banks hold in a checking account at the Fed; bonds are like a savings account at the Fed. When either the Treasury or the Fed sells bonds, it is like switching deposits from the checking account to the saving account. It just lets banks earn higher interest.

Sovereign government bonds are not really for borrowing. They are what Warren calls an interest rate maintenance account. They provide a higher interest-earning alternative to holding reserves. So, much like the relation between taxes and spending – with tax collection coming after spending – we should think of bond sales as occurring after government has already spent the reserves.

In addition, government bond sales lead to reserve debits and bond purchases lead to reserve credits. Treasury spending creates income in the nongovernment sector; taxes reduce income. Bond sales simply change the composition of asset portfolios of the nongovernment sector:

bond holdings increase; reserve holdings decrease. Bond purchases reduce bonds held and increase reserves held. What goes on within the government sector will not change those outcomes, and really should not be of interest to those outside the government.

Government spends by crediting accounts; it doesn't borrow to spend and it doesn't spend tax revenue, either.

3

Can We Have Too Much Money?

Since abandoning the gold standard, there are no physical limits to money creation.[1] We cannot run out of keystroke entries on bank balance sheets – whether we are talking about private banks or the government's central bank. This recognition is fundamental to issues surrounding finance.

As such, the biggest question facing us is this: how can we use finance to promote the capital development[2] of the economy? Finance is not a scarce resource. We can have as much as we want. The problem in recent years has been that our governments wrongly think they're financially constrained, while our private financial system has directed much of its efforts to self-enrichment through speculation rather than to capital development. We will need to reorient our economy so that it serves us well and promotes the public purpose.

To move forward we need to dispel the dual myths that government has run out of money, and that the unfettered invisible hand of private finance will promote the public interest. These myths are not just wrong, they are downright dangerous.

The constraints government faces are not really *financial*. Government does face real resource constraints: it cannot take more than 100 percent of the resources and indeed would cause deprivation of the population long before it removed all of them from private use. It needs to leave enough resources for pursuit of the "private purpose." Political legitimacy will play a role in determining the relative sizes of the public and private spheres. Beyond some point, the population would revolt if it were not left with enough resources to support itself.

How much currency can the government reasonably spend? Well, if the population owes 1,000 currency units in taxes, we know that there will be a demand for currency of at least 1,000 to pay taxes. However, it is likely that the population will accept more currency than that, since people can use it for other purposes. As we know from the case of colonial America, about one-quarter of the issued Virginia paper notes remained in circulation – used by the population in markets as a medium of exchange. Further, if the tax is recurring – say, 1,000 currency units per year – some individuals will want to hold currency to be used to pay taxes in the future. This is using the currency as a store of value – to be spent later.

Recall also that Adam Smith had argued that so long as the issue of paper notes was not too great relative to the tax liability, the notes would retain their value. While that provides a general guide, it is not very specific advice. We need to dig deeper into what determines money's value.

Finally, we will need to come to an agreement on what government should do. National government spending of the rich, developed capitalist economies tends to fall in the range of 25 percent to 50 percent of GDP – with the US at the lower end and France and Scandinavia near the upper end. Arguably, all of them do tolerably well in terms of economic performance, although the US has a far more unequal economy, so it could be argued that it fails to provide decent economic outcomes for those at the bottom. Still, it appears that size of government is largely a political choice – not an economic choice: above some minimum size of government, increasing size doesn't generate a better economy. It comes down to what the population wants government to do, and what it wants to leave to the private sector. We will discuss public policy issues in more detail in chapters 5 through 7.

Here we are going to focus on a big question: what happens if total spending is too great? Here we would include both government spending and private spending. Both types of spending are financed by money creation. What happens if there's just too much money financing too much spending? Well, possibly, *inflation* – prices rise. Looking at it the other way around, the *value* of the currency falls relative to the stuff you want to buy. Let's explore the determinants of the value of money.

A. What Determines the Value of the Currency?

Let's think about those free pizza coupons. As we discussed, they are the liability of the pizza restaurant that issues them, with each coupon entitling the "creditor" to a pizza. These have a fixed "real" value in terms of pizza: one coupon = one pizza. However, such coupons typically have an expiration date, beyond which their value falls to zero.

Does the value of the coupon depend on the number issued? No – so long as the pizza restaurant remains in business and honors its liability, each coupon is worth a pizza no matter how many are issued. Most coupons will probably expire before redemption – which is part of the business model of the issuing restaurant. But those presented before the expiration date can be redeemed at the rate of one coupon per pizza – whether the restaurant issues 100 or 1,000 coupons.

If, however, the restaurant issues too many coupons, it would reduce its revenue from paying customers, and beyond some point might face more redemptions than it could profitably fulfill. There is a real resource constraint

– the restaurant's capacity to produce pizzas – and in addition, a profitability constraint: its ability to earn sufficient revenue to cover its costs, including those of providing the free pizzas. It could always issue more free pizza coupons – it cannot run out of those – but it does face profitability and capacity constraints.

What about the sovereign's currency? Its redemption value is the tax liability. In terms of its ability to pay down tax liabilities, the currency's value is fixed regardless of the number of currency units issued. In this respect the currency functions in the same manner as the pizza coupon: you can always redeem $1 of currency for $1 of taxes due, regardless of the number of dollars that have been issued. And the sovereign's currency never expires![3] Dollars are always "current" (from whence our term "currency" comes).

There are two differences, however. First, pizza coupons generally do not circulate as a general medium of exchange. Yes, you might pass along some coupons to friends, and you might even sell them for cash. (Their cash value would likely be somewhat less than the nominal price of a pizza.) But these are relatively minor exceptions. Currency, of course, does circulate and is an important medium of exchange. Indeed, as we discussed, those colonial paper notes were even preferred by many Americans to British coins as a medium of exchange used in markets.

This leads to the second important difference between pizza coupons and currency. Coupons are generally given away for free (although sometimes "coupon books" are sold with collections of a variety of coupons). Government's currency is generally not just given away. In our simple example above, government spends its currency to obtain real resources used to pursue the public purpose. In other words, the government issues the currency to move resources to the public sector, purchasing what it needs. This is what determines how much currency gets into the economy – how much the government spends (or lends[4]) determines how much currency is supplied.

Now, it "takes two to tango," because for the government to purchase resources, there must be sellers of those resources. That means that there is a second "real" value of the currency, measured in terms of the real resources the currency can buy – in addition to the currency's nominal value in terms of the money of account (what the currency is worth at "government pay houses" where fees, fines, and taxes are paid). This really is what Adam Smith had in mind when he warned against issuing too much currency relative to the tax liability.

In our simple example we assumed that the tax liability is 1,000 and we argued that would create a demand for currency of at least 1,000. Sellers of resources would offer at least 1,000 worth of resources to obtain the currency needed to pay taxes. But they are likely to offer more because the currency can also be used as a medium of exchange and store of value.

How much more? Well, the government could ramp up its spending, going beyond 1,000 as it offered to buy more resources. So long as sellers were willing to sell more resources the government would buy them. Ultimately, it would be the sellers who decided how much currency the government could spend – not the government! Once the sellers obtained all the currency they wanted – to meet tax obligations, to use as a medium of exchange, and to store for future use – they would stop offering resources for sale. When would that point be reached? We cannot say with certainty, but we can be sure it would come before the government bought up all the resources – since the private sector would want some resources for private use. So long as the government was purchasing only "extra" resources not wanted by the private sector, we can presume that willing sellers would come forth.

The tricky question is whether the value of the currency would remain constant in terms of the resources government is buying as it tries to increase its purchases. The answer depends on the government's buying strategy. Let us distinguish between two distinct strategies. In the first one, government decides to pay "whatever it takes" to ensure it can spend 2,000 currency units. We can call this a "fixed quantity/floating price" strategy. The government is going to spend 2,000 (fixed quantity) and will pay whatever price sellers demand (floating price).

The second strategy is a fixed price/floating quantity strategy. The government will not increase the price it pays for any resource it wants to buy, but will buy whatever quantity suppliers offer for sale at the fixed price. Note that this means government might not be able to spend 2,000 – the sellers will determine how much government spends. It should be obvious that the first strategy *could* lead to rising prices paid by government for resources it buys. In other words, the value of the currency could decline relative to the real resources it buys. This is what Adam Smith worried about. We call this inflation. To be sure, we cannot say that spending 2,000 *would* cause inflation, *but it might.*

However, a government that pursues the second strategy will maintain a stable value of the currency by fixing the price it pays for resources. In the terms expressed by Adam Smith, government would always be issuing just the right amount of currency relative to the tax obligations it imposed. In both cases, by imposing a tax the government is creating a demand for its currency, the purpose of which is to move resources to the public sector. The act of spending the currency completes the objective.

By raising the tax obligation (from, say, 1,000 to 2,000) the government will be able to move more resources following either strategy. The fixed price/floating quantity will do so without raising prices (reducing the real value of the currency), even where government's spending is greater than the total tax obligation, since the price paid by government is fixed. When following the fixed price/floating quantity strategy the government sets the tax at the level thought to be consistent with moving the portion of resources required to pursue the public purpose. Government's spending will be determined by sellers willing to sell to government at the fixed price. The tax will determine the *minimum* volume of resources government can move, but the actual volume will likely be higher – and the extra amount will be set by sellers.

With the fixed price/floating quantity approach, it is important to set taxes at a level at least sufficient to generate sale offers equal to the amount of resources government desires to command, but it is not important to match government spending and taxing. Indeed, since government's currency will be demanded for other purposes (a general medium of exchange and store of value), government will expect to spend more currency than it will collect in redemption taxes. In other words, some of the currency will continue to circulate. And it will do so without endangering the value of the currency – relative to both taxes and real resources.

Note: if government spending is greater than taxes, a budget deficit is recorded. Who determines the size of the deficit? In the fixed price/floating quantity approach, the sellers decide – they want more of the government's currency than they need to pay taxes. They are voluntarily deciding to save currency. Hold that thought! We will come back to it.

By contrast, the fixed quantity/floating price strategy is likely to result in inflation beyond some level of resource utilization (and spending). Adam Smith's warning about maintaining the right balance between taxes and note issue is most applicable to this fixed quantity/floating price strategy. That is, it is more important to set tax rates in line with, or even ahead of, spending when pursuing the fixed quantity/floating price strategy. This is because it is possible for inflation to occur even with spending below tax obligations simply because government is willing to raise the price it pays. So the fixed quantity/floating price strategy *could* generate inflation.

By contrast, with the fixed price/floating quantity strategy, the government simply says "NO!" to sellers that demand higher prices – government won't buy at the higher price.

In short, a sovereign government can impose a tax liability and spend its currency to move resources to the public purpose. While it faces resource constraints, it does not face any financial constraints. If it uses a fixed price/floating quantity strategy, its total spending will be determined by the private sector's total demand for the currency – to pay taxes, to use as a medium of exchange, and to act as a store of value. If a deficit occurs, it is because the population wants to accumulate currency beyond what is needed to pay taxes. The value of the currency will remain stable with respect to the tax liabilities and to prices of resources.

Use of a fixed quantity/floating price strategy opens the possibility of inflation (declining purchasing power of the currency). It doesn't guarantee inflation, but it makes inflation possible.

So, in theory, a sovereign shouldn't face any domestic financial constraint – it can simply impose obligations on the population sufficient to move the quantity of resources desired to the government sector, then purchase what it wants with its own currency. But in practice, the ability to impose sufficient obligations might be constrained. What that means is that the sovereign would face *real* constraints: a tax revolt would limit the quantity of real resources that could be moved to the "public purpose" – not because the sovereign would run out of "money" but because the level of taxes imposed wouldn't create a sufficient demand for the currency to allow the sovereign to purchase as many resources as desired. While government *could* spend more, if it is willing to pay higher prices, it can drive prices up and get no more resources.

B. Real-World Constraints

While in theory the monarch's power – including the power to impose taxes and issue currency – might have been absolute, in practice it was limited and faced rivals. Enforcing tax obligations was not always easy. Counterfeiting of the monarch's currency was a constant problem. Subjects sometimes revolted and refused to pay. Or refused to accept the king's coins. (Penalties were severe – ranging from having a red hot coin burned into one's forehead to being put to death.)

And some payments had to be made across borders – to those who owed no taxes to the crown. This was especially problematic during war because the loser's currency might become worthless. In such circumstances, monarchs were sometimes forced to make payments in another authority's currency, or in precious metal bullion. In such cases they might be forced to borrow foreign currency. Medieval Italian bankers became powerful from lending to financially constrained European kings. Moreover, control of the resources needed might be in the hands of powerful rivals to the king's power. Creditors might even want to increase their power over the monarch by putting the king into perpetual indebtedness – bonds that pay interest.

In the late seventeenth century, the first two central banks were formed – first in Sweden and then in Britain. These were created to help finance government's spending. As mentioned earlier, in the case of the British crown, a default on tally sticks had reduced trust. The creation of the Bank of England by Parliament relieved the crisis even as it exerted some Parliamentary control over the king's finances. Over the next couple of hundred years, the West developed the institutional arrangements that we are familiar with today: democratic control over budgeting, a treasury that is charged with spending and taxing, and a central bank that facilitates payments from and to the treasury. In addition, the central bank has been charged with facilitating private payments, and with regulating and supervising private financial institutions.

In the real world, before spending more, government needs to consider whether resources are available for purchase. As we will discuss later, if there are unemployed resources, government can safely put them to use – it is a "free lunch." If there aren't sufficient unemployed resources, government will need to reduce the private sector's use of resources in order to free up some for public use. We'll discuss how the government can use taxes and other strategies for reducing private use. Government's price policy is also important: setting the price government is willing to pay for resources will be less inflationary than chasing prices up in a bidding war against the private sector. Finally, of course, politics will play a role. Government will need to build support for its proposed programs – which need to be budgeted (funds allocated) and resourced (resources mobilized for the project). We will address this later.

C. Can We Ever Have Too Much Money?

We have alluded to the fear surrounding money. One of the greatest fears is that "too much money causes inflation." What is to stop government and banks from creating too much? Furthermore, what is the relation between money creation and financial crises? Didn't we just go through a global financial crisis (GFC) that began around 2008 – and wasn't it caused by excessive money creation?

Let's examine the problems with "too much" money.

As we have seen, Hyman Minsky said "Everyone can create money"; but "the problem is to get it accepted." Money is by nature an IOU. You can create a dollar-denominated "money" by writing "IOU five dollars" on a slip of paper. Your problem is to get someone to accept it.

Sovereign government has an easy time finding acceptors – in part because millions of us owe tax payments to government – or our creditors do.

Bank of America and Citibank also have an easy time finding acceptors of their IOUs – in part because millions of us owe loan payments to Bank of America or Citibank, in part because we know we can exchange deposits at our bank for cash, and in part because we know the Fed stands behind the banks to ensure par clearing with any other bank.

While there is some justified fear that runaway money creation would diminish the value of our money, the risk is usually overstated by people who do not understand how money gets created.

Banks create money when they make loans. Banks are constrained – or should be constrained – by the supply of potential borrowers who are creditworthy and willing to borrow. Proper oversight and regulation by authorities can keep banks in check. Note that when a bank does lend to a creditworthy borrower, the money it creates (in the form of demand deposits) will be redeemed. That is, it will be removed from the economy as the loan is repaid – indeed, as it will be repaid with interest, the redemption will *exceed* the original amount!

When an economy is doing well, private banks will be expanding loans and creating new deposits. Private spending will be rising. This will induce firms to produce more goods and services. There is no reason to believe this will necessarily cause prices to rise: both demand and supply of output will be rising. Further, as demand for output is rising, firms will likely invest more in plant and equipment and will hire more workers – so potential output will rise. While there could be pressure on prices, that pressure could be in either the upward (rising prices) or downward (falling prices) direction – depending on whether demand is rising faster than, or slower than, capacity to provide output.

As loans and deposits grow, and as the economy grows, money will be created and also destroyed through redemption (loan repayment). At any point in time we can measure the "money stock" (the total of all deposits outstanding at that moment).[5] Essentially what we would be measuring is the total deposits created by bank lending that had not yet been used to retire loans. Many economists used to think that the money stock was a very important variable, closely linked to spending and inflation. Indeed, there was a period when the Fed tried to control the rate of growth of the money stock – from 1979 to 1982. However, today no competent central banker believes that the money stock should be targeted, or that changes to the money stock provide much information about economic performance or inflation pressure. Today, central banks target interest rates. (We are not going to delve more deeply into lingering misunderstanding about the importance of measuring the "money supply.")

Let's turn briefly to the possibility that too much government money might be inflationary. As we've seen, sovereign government spends by crediting bank reserves, with banks crediting deposit accounts. Hence, deposits also go up when government spends. Taxes reverse that, with deposits and reserves debited – that is, taxes redeem government currency (today almost always in the form of reserves). Uncle Sam is subject to the budget authority that is provided by Congress and approved by the President. We hold them accountable at the ballot box.

Democratic governance is not perfect but works better than the alternatives. There aren't any examples of democratic countries whose money was destroyed by overissue. Those few examples that seem to qualify prove on closer inspection to have had a number of unusual circumstances that contributed to currency problems – it was not a simple matter of government creating "too much money"; rather there were usually significant political problems and supply-side problems. People get hung up on the supposed role of government *money* creating inflation – but there is no direct link. The danger is that government *spending* can be inflationary if the government continues to bid higher prices to take resources away from private use. This is a common experience during major wars – but World War II demonstrated that governments can reduce price pressures by adopting a variety of measures such as encouraging patriotic saving, increasing taxes, imposing wage and price controls, and rationing.

Many people incorrectly believe that only "money-financed" government spending would be inflationary – but as we have explained, all government spending today takes the same form: a credit by the central bank to a bank's reserves, and the bank's credit to the demand deposit of the recipient. And this is true no matter what the budgetary outcome might be (surplus, deficit, balance) at the end of the accounting period. So it is not money's fault, but rather too much spending at ever higher prices (floating price case). If government always spent on a fixed price/floating quantity basis, its spending would not be directly inflationary.

It is spending, not money, that creates inflation pressure. Let's try a mental experiment. Assume the government prints gazillions of dollars and sends them to Mars. No inflation. Then Elon Musk flies a spaceship to Mars, brings back the money and starts spending like a whirling dervish. Inflation. Blame the spending, not the money.

D. Private Money Creation and Financial Instability

As we've seen, private spending, financed by bank money creation, *could* be inflationary. However, the greater danger of "too much money creation" by banks is typically *not* inflation, but rather financial crisis. Too much *private* money often means too much risky debt. The risks build until a crisis erupts.

This typically involves lending to purchase financial assets. If asset prices are rising, it seems reasonable to borrow to purchase assets on the expectation that they can be sold later at a higher price. If that expectation proves valid, the loans can be repaid easily, with profits left over. This is called speculation, and using borrowed funds is called leverage. If you put in ten bucks of your own money and borrow ninety your potential gains are multiplied if asset prices do rise. You can repay the loans plus interest and walk away with profits on the borrowed money as well as on your own equity. Of course, if your expectations were wrong, you not only make losses on your equity but also must repay loans and interest. It is a risky business.

To be sure, the markets do not see it that way – expansions make it easy to be successful, so leveraging up debt does not seem risky. We recognize the increased risk mostly *ex post*, when a few bets go wrong and we begin to worry about our own finances. The combination of rising leverage and increasingly complex financial linkages ensures that a few sufficiently large failures will quickly ripple through the entire financial system. Liquidity suddenly disappears.

Losses compound very quickly. Let's say that aluminum (used in beer cans and airplanes) prices are rising rapidly. You leverage up and buy aluminum on credit (you'll probably buy futures contracts, not actual aluminum, but we are not focusing on those details). Some speculators start to believe aluminum prices are too high and bound to fall. They start selling – driving prices down. Even if you believe they might be wrong, you begin to worry about all that debt you owe, so you and everyone else start selling and the price collapses. Your creditors demand payment, forcing you to sell other kinds of assets; others do the same. The dynamics are perverse: everyone is selling assets because prices are falling, and the sales drive prices ever lower.

This is what Irving Fisher called a "debt deflation" process,[6] and he explained that this is what caused the Great Depression of the 1930s to be so "great." This has been repeated on a somewhat smaller scale over the past few decades, with the GFC that began in 2008 as the best and biggest example. Since the 1930s, we've avoided another great depression, largely through government intervention with both fiscal policy (spending) and monetary policy (lending).

In a debt deflation scenario, the only liquid and safe assets are currency and bank reserves, as well as sovereign government bonds. In the old days, this would trigger runs on banks (you may recall the scene in *It's a Wonderful Life* when Jimmy Stewart's character implores his customers to keep their deposits in his bank). Today we have deposit insurance, so the run is only on uninsured bank liabilities. The run to liquidity can only be stopped by central bank intervention as "lender of last resort," lending its reserves to banks so they can meet cash withdrawals. The basic rule of thumb is to "lend without limit" against assets that would be good if we were not in a crisis. In the aftermath of the GFC, the Fed went further. It dropped its target interest rate to near zero; it lent against questionable assets; and it bought trillions of dollars of assets, including not only Treasury bonds but also private debt such as mortgage-backed securities (this was called quantitative easing)

Fiscal policy can take the form of "stimulus": temporary government spending programs (or tax relief). The Obama administration spent approximately $800 billion over a two-year period trying to lift the economy out of the recession brought on by the GFC. The global COVID-19 pandemic generated an even deeper recession and led to several rounds of "relief" packages – that had totaled about $5 trillion in the case of the USA by the end of 2021.

The upside of such interventions is that we have – so far – avoided another great depression. The downside is that every intervention by government (including lender-of-last-resort rescues by the central bank) validates the behavior that helped to create the crisis (by preventing widespread bankruptcies of financial institutions). That is, successful rescues promote more risk-taking. Economists call this the problem of "moral hazard": knowing that Uncle Sam will bail you out virtually ensures you'll need the bailout. This makes the structure of the economy evolve toward greater fragility.

This is precisely what Minsky presciently predicted would happen over the postwar period.[7] He began to develop what he called the "financial instability hypothesis" in the late 1950s. The early postwar period was unusually quiescent– there were no significant financial crises between World War II and the mid-1960s. Minsky attributed this to financial regulation plus subdued risk-taking maintained due to memories of the Great Depression. No one who lived through that fiasco wanted to take excessive risk. But he predicted that memories would fade, that financial institutions would find ways to get around the regulations, and that financial practices would eventually evolve to promote more risk. And if the government (especially the Fed and FDIC) intervened to prevent crisis, those risky behaviors would be encouraged.

This is why Minsky always said that his financial instability hypothesis is fundamentally pessimistic. That doesn't mean you give up – and Minsky was optimistic by nature. What he meant was that while you can never provide a once-and-for-all solution to financial instability, you can constrain the instability through apt policy. Because there is no final solution, policy must be continually revised, and policy makers must be diligent. You want them to lend to promote the capital development of the economy without promoting speculative bubbles. And you need to punish bad behavior.

In sum, what is the danger of too much money creation by private banks? Well, they *could* finance excessive spending and increase the danger of inflation. This is similar to the problem of too much government spending leading to excessive demand on the nation's resources and output. But there is another danger when it comes to private money creation: financial instability. Financial crises are usually the result of too much money creation by private financial institutions. And, as mentioned, they usually result from lending to purchase assets, including houses. This then boosts prices of the assets and can generate bubbles. The GFC was preceded by bubbles in the housing market, commodities, and dot-com stocks. In every case, borrowed money helped to fuel the bubble. In recent years, it appears that such crises have become more common and much more serious. It also has become harder for the government to prevent deep and long-lived economic downturns that can be set off by financial crises.

So, as we study how the monetary system works, we need to heed Minsky's warning that our financial system is not necessarily benign. Left to its own devices, it does not serve us well. We need to take stock of the true risks even as we begin to understand why so many fears about money are ill-founded.

E. Conclusions

Private bank money creation is limited by rules of thumb, underwriting standards, capital ratios, and other imposed constraints. Central bank reserve (money) creation is only limited by what it perceives to be necessary to keep the payments system functioning smoothly – so that both government and private checks clear – and to stop any bank run before it spreads too far (e.g. to protected liabilities such as deposits).

The upshot is that we cannot run out of keystroke entries on bank balance sheets. This recognition is fundamental to issues surrounding finance. It is also a bit scary.

The good thing about the ability of banks and the central bank to create money is that sufficient finance can always be supplied to fully utilize all available resources to support the capital development of the economy. We can keystroke our way to full employment. The bad thing about the ability to create money is that we can create more funding than we can reasonably use in the productive sphere. Further, our bankers might make bad choices about which activities ought to get keystroked finance. It is difficult to find examples of excessive money creation to finance productive uses. Rather, the main problem is that much of the money creation is related to financing nonproductive asset purchases, which can fuel asset price bubbles.

The biggest challenge facing us today is *not* the lack of finance, but rather how to push finance to promote both the private and the public interest.

4

Balances Balance

In this chapter we build on our understanding of monetary matters.[1] Previously we have argued that money is always issued as a debt (liability) and held by someone who accepts it as an asset (credit). In the aggregate, monetary assets equal monetary liabilities; credits equal debits. They must balance. This is by identity.

But what if balance were something that *might not* occur automatically? Something we'd like to achieve, but that might require a push by a knowing, yet perhaps invisible, impulse? Maybe an invisible hand of market or God?

In conventional economics there is the notion that balance is achieved by the invisible hand of the market, which adjusts prices until the quantity supplied equals the quantity demanded. That is "balance," called "equilibrium" by orthodox economists. In this chapter, we'll take a look at the notion of balance – which predates economics.

A. Time, Money, and Balance

Many link economics to eighteenth- or nineteenth-century physics with its notion of *equilibrium*, of a pendulum once disturbed eventually coming to rest.[2] Likewise, an economy subjected to an exogenous shock seeks equilibrium through the stabilizing market forces unleashed by the market's invisible hand. Balance may not be automatic, but it is supposedly natural. Leave the economy alone, and it will return to balance – pushed there by the pursuit of individual self-interest.

The equilibrium metaphor has been applied to virtually every sphere of economics: from microeconomic markets for fish that are traded in the local fishmonger market, to national markets for labor, and on to complex financial markets in synthetic and esoteric CDOs (the collateralized debt obligations that helped to blow up the global economy in 2008). Guided by invisible hands, supplies are supposed to balance demands at equilibrium prices so all markets clear. You've no doubt been told that economics is all about demand and supply – the two blades of the scissors. Free markets establish the price at the point where the blades cross.

Armed with metaphors from physics, the economist has no problem extending the analysis across international borders to traded commodities, to what are euphemistically called capital flows, and on to currency exchange rates. Certainly there is a price, somewhere, someplace, somehow, that will balance supply and demand – for the physical goods we can drop on our feet to break a toe, and on to the mental and physical efforts of our brethren, and finally to notional derivatives like credit default swaps that occupy neither time nor space. If there is a demand, and a supply, markets will do their magic if they are left alone.

Balance is nice; it's intuitively appealing. In truth, it was invented neither by physics nor even by humans. It is the universal condition – both in nature and in human society. It reflects an inner yearning for fairness. As Margaret Atwood[3] explains, all human and ape societies have recognized the law of reciprocity – you will pay back in this life (or the next!). There is an innate notion of equivalent values, and therefore of balances. Animals can tell "bigger than" and they revolt when they are shorted; even the rat knows it's not fair – she goes on strike if you try to reduce the usual reward for running a maze. That violates the rodent's notion of balance.

There is a right way to do things. Failure to follow tradition upsets the balance. Who knows what wrath imbalance might invoke among the gods! In Christian tradition, Gabriel, the angel of records, keeps God's ledger book – to be produced in the Last Judgment. Too much imbalance in your life and you go to hell. And, as we know, Lucifer records the debts – of the souls he will collect. He'll sell you a good time now, but your soul lies in the balance. You buy now, you pay forever.

The only things in life you cannot escape are death and taxes. As Atwood explains, the Devil has a lock on both of those. He's the tax collector who calls at death. Once your soul is sold, there is no balance. It's the roach motel – you've checked in and you will never get out. But Christ is said to be the redeemer – he's a sin eater, repaying your debts to restore balance, to let sinners get to heaven. If they repent, Jesus can get them into heaven.

Saint Nick, patron saint of thieves and pawnshops, red-suited and covered in black soot after sliding down the chimney, might just remind you of that other red-suited and sooted bottom-dweller. Both keep lists and check who's been naughty and nice. Gifts and heaven for the virtuous, the naughty get stiffed. As Atwood says, you might catch Saint Nick in your house with a bulging thief's bag and an implausible story about elves at the North Pole. In the nineteenth century, the Devil was referred to as "Old Nick," and "to nick" means to steal – hence the pawnshop. The earliest pawnshops seem to have been in Mesopotamia and were used to pawn kids and wives, in return for cash to repay debts.[4] Old Nick offers an alternative: sell your soul.

Muslims refer to the scales of justice – your good deeds are weighed against the bad ones. There is a balancing out – if you've been good, you might just tip the scales. Much earlier, the God of Time was a Scribe as well as the God of Measurement and Engineering – how would you like that job description? He kept the records, measured worth, and built the scales. At death, he weighed your heart to assess your value.

Interestingly, the Christian pope or pontiff came out of the engineering *gens* (family, clan) of one of the Tribes of Rome – that built all the bridges, or *pontes*, over the Tiber and that became the priestly upper class. John Henry has argued that the engineers who built the canals in ancient Egypt probably became the religious rulers at the dawn of civilization.[5] Their *gens* controlled the flows and were able to convince others that it was their special relationship with the gods that enabled them to deliver the precious life-giving water.

So it is not such a stretch to link record-keeping, measurement, and engineering with the rise of civilization itself. Time, measurement, balance, and authority. Everything you need for money and accounting.

Philip Grierson – a famous numismatologist (coin expert) – argued that the origins of money can be found in the practice of *wergild*. In tribal society, to prevent blood feuds, a system of fines was created in which anyone who perpetrated an injury would have to compensate the victim (or family in the case of wrongful death).[6] Tribal society had no money but would have a list of the appropriate fines for every possible infraction – a goat for cutting off an arm, a horse for murder. (Interestingly, in tribal Russia, cutting off a beard was considered a more serious crime than cutting off an arm – hence, it carried a more valuable fine.)

In other words, fines were paid "in kind" by delivering something readily available and useful. This is where the "bride price" (gifts paid to the family of a bride) practice comes from: the husband was not purchasing a wife but rather was compensating her family for the loss of a woman who had been helping to support the family. The list of fines was established in public assemblies (democratically) and a designated "rememberer" would memorize them (tribal society did not have writing).

While we cannot know for sure, Grierson hypothesized that with the rise of civilization and religious authorities, the fines gradually came to be paid to the priests rather than to the victims. This might have led to the creation of a single unit of account to measure the severity of the crime, and hence, the value of the fine to be paid. As Grierson said, this required a great intellectual leap – it is relatively easy to come up with the inch or foot to measure length, but hard to come up with an abstract unit to measure things that were not obviously commensurate. Originally this was probably an existing grain unit – all the money units were derived from grain measures used for volume. Taking something like the mina or shekel and assigning values to things like goats and sheep made it easy to assess fines in minas for transgressions, paid in kind at the mina values assigned.

The Christian notion of original sin ensured collection of tithes without any specific infractions (we are all guilty from birth) and over the centuries that became fees, fines, and taxes paid to the secular authorities. And the development of writing enabled record-keeping and the creation of the "Devil's" ledger – kept in money values. Prices in money values of all the important commodities were then posted on temple columns, and taxes were originally paid in kind. The final step was to issue money records (clay tablets, wooden sticks, coins, and paper money) to purchase what authorities desired, and accept these in payment of redemption taxes. This would finally replace in-kind payments denominated in a money of account with payment made directly in money form (the record of a money debt issued by the authority).

The rest, as they say, is history.

B. Debt Cancellation and the Soddy Principle

From time immemorial, debts would be periodically cancelled. In Judaic tradition this happened in the Year of Jubilee, which happened after seven cycles of seven years. In other ancient Near Eastern societies it happened with every change of ruler (who, of course, was an earthly God of Measurement – we measure with the Ruler's ruler!). Babylonia chose thirty years as the likely reign of a ruler and so cancelled debts every thirty years; the Bible chose seven times seven – the lucky number, as a seven-year ever-normal granary (a stockpile of grain) would get you through a long drought.

Debt cancellation. Why? These earthly rulers were no bleeding heart liberals. Nay, debt cancellation was to restore balance – in the king's favor.[7] If all your subjects are in hock to creditors, you cannot rule them. So you eat their sins, redeem their debts, free them and their wives and kids from debt bondage. Hallelujah!

Why do we need periodic debt cancellation? The Soddy principle:[8] compound interest "trumps" compound growth (in other words, debts grow faster than ability to pay them, which is constrained by economic growth). Humans recognized this even before they invented writing. The earliest textbooks showed how to calculate compound interest.[9] And interest rates were almost always higher than the growth rate of income[10] – so that indebtedness grows too fast to be paid.

It was our first imbalance – interest rates above growth rates – society's first violation of natural law. It would inevitably lead to concentration of wealth – like the game of Monopoly, where rents increase geometrically while aggregate income increases only arithmetically, ensuring the game will come to an end as the last player standing will take all. So, from Babylonia until Rome, balance was restored by periodically cancelling debts.

With cancellation, the pawned wives and children were set free to return to families. Hallelujah, free at last!

All early societies saw time as circular: beginning with the rise of an emperor and renewed at his death with the rise of a new emperor, when time and accounts would be reset at zero and the slate wiped clean. Time and debt are inherently related. Time compounds the debts at the rate of interest. Heaven is timeless and debt free; in hell all debts are compounded forever.

Redemption Day allows time and debt to start over from balanced accounts. But with Roman law we abolished circular time as we strengthened property relations. Henceforth time moved in one direction only – from a largely known past to an uncertain future. No more debt cancellations. No more clean slates. No more restoration of balance.

Just debtors' prisons – where the debtor would be held until family could redeem him by paying the debts to restore balance. Debtors' prisons destroyed the balance between creditors and the sovereign – just as debt bondage had several thousand years earlier in Babylonia. With the family head in prison, it was impossible to repay the creditor. And with the families in hock to the creditors, they could not serve their king.[11]

Enter bankruptcy from stage left. Like debt cancellation, bankruptcy was invented not out of compassion but to restore the balance between the rights of rulers and of creditors. Yet bankruptcy only allowed a partial reset. It was a poor substitute for Jubilee and Hallelujah. So the creditors still ran the show. They liked inequality; they liked imbalance.

As Kenneth Boulding[12] used to say, surveys of the rich consistently show that you cannot imagine how incredibly greedy they are, and how monumentally short-sighted they are, too. They will gleefully roast the goose that lays the golden egg.

If you do not believe that, you have not been watching Wall Street over the past two decades. Or what Germany did to Greece, Spain, and Italy during the Euro area's government debt crisis. When creditors have too much power, they destroy the balance. More recently, we have the example of the rich nations that kept COVID-19 vaccines from the rest of the world – ensuring the virus would continue to mutate into ever more dangerous strains. That's the *bad karma* payback as the new strains invade the rich countries.

C. Government Debt and Balance

Let's bring this up to the present. Credit and debt are two sides of the same coin. Both creditor and debtor are sinful. They balance. Exactly. The balance is ensured by double-entry book-keeping. The debtor's debt is equal to the creditor's asset. Penny for penny. Pound for pound. Redemption frees both creditor and debtor. It results in a different balance – one without sin. Bankruptcy also results in a kind of balance, but one that maintains the power of creditor over debtor – at least within the limits of law.

Figure 1 shows the sectoral balances for the USA. The upper graphed line is the nongovernment sector and the lower graphed line is the government sector. Note that the nongovernment sector includes the domestic private sector (households and firms) plus the "rest of the world" (the balance of all other countries against the US). The government sector includes both the federal government and state and local governments. This is at the level of the economy as a whole and shows income minus spending. If a sector spends less than its income it will have a surplus – above zero. If it spends more than its income it will have a deficit – below zero.

You can see that the US government sector is almost always in the "red" (that is, below the zero line), meaning in deficit, with spending greater than income. While state and local governments are included, they normally

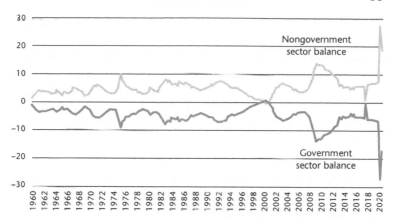

Figure 1 Government and nongovernment sector balances (% of GDP) 1960–2020

run surpluses – so it is the federal government's usually large deficits that push the lower graphed line below zero. On the other hand, the nongovernment sector (upper graphed line) is almost always above the line, in surplus, with spending less than income. The common term for a surplus is "saving": the nongovernment sector saves. US households almost always save (spend less than income); US business sometimes run surpluses and other times run deficits (for example, when they borrow to finance investment spending); and the foreign sector has run a surplus (saving dollars) against the US since the days of President Reagan.[13]

The point is this: debts and credits are always in balance. In the private sector, as we say, "inside" debts (that is, debts of one in the private sector to another in the private sector) net to zero. Balance. But our domestic private sector accumulates financial wealth in the form of claims on the other sectors. Since the US runs a current account deficit, it is the rest of the world that accumulates dollar-denominated savings that are claims on the US government and the US private sector. Hence, positive savings of our domestic private sector require that our government sector run a deficit. The government's deficit must be big enough to cover the domestic private sector surplus, plus the foreign sector's surplus (our current account deficit).

In normal times, the private sector surplus plus the current account deficit equal the budget deficit. In the abnormal times of private sector deficits (the decade that preceded the GFC), we still saw balance – the government ran budget surpluses for a few years during the Clinton administration to maintain the balance, with the private sector deficit equaling the government surplus added to the foreign sector's surplus. This means that our private sector had to run deficits to let our government as well as foreigners run surpluses.

Hilariously, the federal government surplus was celebrated by the US media and officialdom in Washington as a great success, supposedly adding to the nation's savings. At the same time, the private sector's deficit was said to be shameful, subtracting from the nation's savings. In 1999, the *Wall Street Journal* even published a helpful front page showing a graph of government saving (turning positive by 1998) and private saving (turning negative) – with separate stories covering each. (See figure 2, which presents the same data. The upper graphed line shows the annual personal savings rate, and the lower graphed line shows the deficit or surplus as a percentage of GDP.) Remarkably, neither

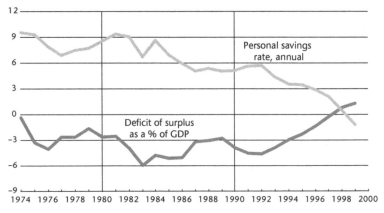

Figure 2 Government surpluses mean private deficits

of the stories referenced the other one. The fact that the two sectors' balances are related through an identity was never recognized.

Indeed, given a US current account deficit, if the government is to run a surplus, the private sector *must be* running a deficit, *by accounting identity*. Such is the sorry state of economics that the premier US media outlet for economic news – the *Wall Street Journal* – does not understand that balances balance!

President Clinton even appeared on TV at the time and announced that the US government would run surpluses for the next fifteen years, eliminating all the government debt! While he didn't state it, this would have implied that the US private sector likely would have run deficits[14] over the same period, accumulating trillions of dollars of net indebtedness. Needless to say, it didn't happen. The budget surpluses lasted just over two years as the private sector's debt grew and then the economy crashed into a recession because excessive spending by households ran out of steam. We've had annual government deficits ever since. So much for Clinton's prediction.

There is always financial balance. Imbalance can arise only due to arithmetic errors. Looking at our global mess as a financial imbalance – as almost everyone does – is a mistake. Neither the US government budget deficit nor the US trade deficit represents a dangerous imbalance. They are balanced as the graphs demonstrate. To the penny. The government's deficit allows the private sector to save – and the saving is in the safest asset on planet earth: claims on the US government.

The trade balance balances too! Our current account deficit equals the rest of the world's current account surplus. We get the stuff they export to us, and they get US dollars. It balances.

D. Money and Sovereign Power

We need to look at financial balances the way Babylonia's rulers saw them. When the population's debts got too big, the rulers declared a general debt cancellation. This was to restore the balance of power. Our problem today is with the balance of power, not a financial imbalance. Our global financial elites have too much power. The rest of the population – as well as Uncle Sam, himself – has too little. And to understand this, we've got to understand what money is.

To greatly simplify, as we have argued above, money is a measuring unit, originally created by rulers to value the fees, fines, and taxes owed to the rulers. By putting the subjects or citizens into debt – a sort of original sin – real resources could be moved to serve the public purpose. Taxes (and other obligations to the rulers) drive money. This is why money is always linked to sovereign power – the power to command resources. That power is rarely absolute. It is contested, with other sovereigns, but often more important is the contest with domestic creditors. Too much debt to private creditors reduces sovereign power – it destroys the balance of power needed to govern.

Debt cancellation can restore the balance of power – just as it did in Babylonia.

Money was created to give government command over some of the socially created resources. It did not come out of private markets but rather was created as a means of moving resources to the rulers. We can think of money as the currency of taxation, with the money of account denominating one's social liability.

I have to deliver a dollar's worth of commodities – including labor hours – to satisfy the public interest. In return, I receive money to pay the tax. Often, it is the tax that monetizes an activity – that puts a money value on it for the purpose of determining the share to "render unto Caesar" – as the Bible says.[15]

The sovereign government names what money-denominated record (whether that takes the form of a wooden tally stick, a clay "shubati" tablet, a metal coin, or a paper note) can be delivered in redemption against one's social obligation to pay taxes. It can then issue the money record in its own payments. That government money record is, like all money things, a liability denominated in the state's money of account. And like all money records, it must be redeemed, that is, accepted by its issuer. Clearly, it's not money that the sovereign wants – it wants real resources. Money receipts are the tool, not the goal. The sovereign issues its money to you to get the resources you can supply to it; you use that money to pay your obligation. It is your obligation to pay taxes that induces you to work for the sovereign's money.

But if you are burdened by excessive debt to private creditors, you work to get money to pay them. By the end of the day, you are too exhausted to work to provide the resources the sovereign needs. If private creditors run the economy there just isn't enough power to produce left for the sovereign – for the public purpose. Government has an unlimited supply of its own money – but there have to be available productive resources for it to purchase.

In modern economies that is not the usual constraint, however. Government's sovereign power is typically constrained in two main ways: arbitrary self-imposed budgetary constraints, and exchange rate constraints. Many countries happily impose both types – including Euroland. The handcuffs of budget limits were not enough – so they imposed the ball and chain of the Euro. We observed the fallout after the GFC, which pitted Euro nation against Euro nation, and with forced austerity on any country that was not Germany or the Netherlands (the two major exporters – which had massive claims against the rest of the Euro area; Finland and Luxembourg also had small surpluses).

The problem is not a financial imbalance but rather an imbalance of power. Germany and the Netherlands have too much; the GIIPS (Greece, Italy, Ireland, Portugal, and Spain) have too little. You can curse the moon for its travels but it still is going to circumnavigate the globe. Admonish the Mediterraneans all you like for their budget deficits, but they still will have them, compounded by the German export surpluses.

Can anyone say "debt cancellation" to restore the balance between creditor and debtor nations?

A sovereign government that issues its own currency faces no financial constraints. It cannot produce a financial imbalance. It can buy any resources that are for sale in terms of its own currency by using keystrokes. Its debt is the private sector's asset, and the resources can be mobilized in the public interest through those keystrokes. That does not mean government should try to buy all the resources it can – too much buying can certainly produce inflation while leaving too few resources to fulfill the private purpose. Government needs to use its sovereign power to move just the right amount of resources to serve the public purpose while leaving enough for the private purpose. That balance is mostly political. It is hard to find, as we discuss later.

Imposing an arbitrary budget limit or supposed "balance" between tax receipts and government spending is the worst possible way of trying to find the right balance between the public and private purposes. What it usually does is leave the resources unused – wasted – rather than leave them for the private purpose. It is much better to explicitly decide: what do we want government to do? What do we want our private sector to do? Do we have a sufficient supply of resources domestically plus what we can obtain externally through imports to achieve both? If we don't, how can we expand capacity as needed?

We are not arguing for a planned economy as usually defined. But of course, all economies are planned, of necessity. There is no chance that something like a system as complicated as the modern economy could function without planning. The question is *by whom and for whom*. In recent years, the planning has been taken over by multinational corporations, especially by financial behemoths pursuing their own narrow self-interests. Sovereign governments have given over much of their power to them, largely in the misguided belief that the governments, themselves, are short of money.

These are the real issues; they are difficult; they are contentious. But they have almost nothing to do with the size of a budget deficit. It is worse than pointless to set a deficit ratio goal of 3 percent or 6 percent, and a debt ratio goal of 60 percent – as Euroland did, to try to achieve some preconceived notion of balance. It is counterproductive. Finances balance. No matter how much someone might protest.

E. Sovereignty and Exchange Rates

Let's turn to the other common self-imposed constraint: pegged exchange rates. Adopting a gold standard, or a foreign currency standard ("dollarization" or "Euro-ization," where your country's exchange rate is fixed against either the dollar or the Euro), or for that matter Milton Friedman's[16] money growth rule, or an inflation target, is a political act that serves the interests of some privileged group.

There is no "natural" separation of a government from its money. The gold standard was legislated, just as the Federal Reserve Act of 1913 legislated the separation of Treasury and Central Bank functions, and the (US) Balanced Budget Act of 1987 legislated the *ex ante* matching of federal government spending and revenue. More recently, the US Congress has imposed on itself "pay-go" requirements: spending proposals must be matched either by a reduction of spending elsewhere, or by a tax increase. All of these are self-imposed – like tying your shoelaces together before starting a marathon.

Ditto the myth of the supposed independence of the modern central bank – this is only a self-imposed smokescreen to hide the fact that monetary policy is biased in favor of finance operating on Wall Street and in London and Frankfurt and Paris. The central bank is the government's bank. The Fed is legally a "creature of Congress" – Congress created it in the Federal Reserve Act, which has been amended several times – and Congress can (and should) ensure the Fed operates in the public interest. All it takes is a Congressional mandate.

These efforts at balance are superfluous. Imbalance of finance is impossible. Imbalance of power is the result of these misguided efforts.

Pegging your nation's exchange rate to another nation's currency surrenders your currency sovereignty to that country. You essentially become their colony. You lose control over both fiscal and monetary power and expose your nation to the triple threat of exchange rate crises, national insolvency, and bankruptcy. As Wynne Godley said: "[T]he power to issue its own money, to make drafts on its own central bank, is the main thing which defines national independence. If a country gives up or loses this power, it acquires the status of a local authority or colony."[17] If a nation pegs its currency, it must hope to export on a sufficient scale to obtain the foreign currency that will protect the exchange rate and allow it to service its debt. In other words, the nation must work hard to produce output it cannot enjoy, all in the service of its chosen colonizer that issues the dominant currency. If your colonizer is benevolent, you might enjoy a stable exchange rate and maybe a decent living standard. Throughout history, unfortunately, colonizers have not proven to be very benevolent – which is why the colonized have revolted. Sooner or later.[18]

And once a new nation is formed it almost always chooses its own, new, money. To shift the balance of power in its favor.

F. Conclusion: A World Out of Balance

If you take the world as a whole, there is no external sector since we don't trade with Martians (yet?). And so the sum of the global government deficits equals the sum of the private sector surpluses. It balances. The real imbalance is power. And this isn't just a European disease. There is a generalized perception of a world out of balance. We've had Arab Springs, Occupy Wall Street movements, MAGA ("make America great again") in the US, and protests all over Europe. The Brits got Brexit. And the US was Trumped as voters rejected the mainstream candidates of both parties and elected a narcissistic reality TV star. Not long ago, Italian voters actually chose a clown to lead the country. Now country after country in Europe is toying with bringing back the Fascists. America has its own home-grown fascists.

Why? Imbalances: all over the Western world the public sector is too small; we've privatized too many essential public sector functions – our arts, culture, prisons and punishment, military in Afghanistan and Iraq, increasingly our education and healthcare, even our motor vehicle departments. All are increasingly privatized. Even responsibility for full employment was shunted off to the private sector as governments downgraded the role of fiscal policy for economic stabilization. Supervision of our banks also fell by the wayside – we let them self-regulate, and even self-prosecute, self-punish, and self-flagellate when fraud and other criminal behavior were uncovered.

What happens when government abandons its proper role? At the top, we get fraud. Corruption. Gross incompetence. For the rest of us? We get unemployment, inequality, poverty, and inadequate healthcare, retirement, and welfare.

If you think about it we chose the worst of all possible times to embark on the great neoliberal experiment –

downsizing government, privatizing many of its functions, slashing the safety net. Because in the wealthy nations of the West we are aging rapidly – which creates the twin problems of the need to devote more resources to aged care and at the same time a private desire to accumulate financial resources for individual retirements. Attempts to increase private saving can reduce demand and hinder economic growth. That makes it hard to build up the resources we need to care for the aged.

At the same time, the attempt to accumulate funds for retirement led to the accumulation of unprecedented financial wealth under management by Wall Street's professionals. Current and future retirees demanded higher returns to increase their security and Wall Street responded by pulling more resources into the financial sector, doubling its share of value added and capturing 40 percent of all corporate profits. It's too much.

Finance is an intermediate good that might in the best of circumstances contribute to production by financing useful activities. But finance largely services itself – ever on the hunt for some new asset class to bubble up. With attention diverted to Wall Street, we didn't increase our ability to care for an aging population.

At the same time, financial wealth represents a potential claim on output but does not guarantee output will be available as needed. We need old folks' homes but finance is more interested in gambling on CDOs (fancy virtual reality derivatives that place bets that homeowners will lose their homes) squared and cubed. And it is worse than that. Modern finance, at least what is practiced at the biggest banks, is largely about fraud. So, finance is not even a zero-sum game – it makes a large negative economic contribution.[19]

The imbalance is one of power – not government deficits. The disease is excessive financialization of our economy. The symptoms are the subprime frauds in the US, the austerity imposed on Greece and Iceland, the stagnation of incomes in most developed nations, the rising inequality and poverty in the midst of plenty, the growing despair and feelings of hopelessness.

There are no quick fixes, no magic bullets. The solution is not to slash government spending in Greece. Even reform of Maastricht rules plus bigger bailouts is not a solution. We don't need another Dodd–Frank reform of the financial system. Not even a return of Glass–Steagall separation of investment banks from commercial banks would do much good. No, the reforms must be fundamental. And they must begin with a better understanding of money.

5
Life Is Full of Trade-Offs

A. Private Trade-Offs

Our personal experience teaches us that life is full of trade-offs. Should I study for my calculus exam, or go to the movies? I'll enjoy the movie tremendously more than studying, but if I fail the exam, I might not graduate. Should I take an expensive vacation to the Bahamas, or put the money into my IRA (individual retirement account)? Retirement is a long way off and the vacation sure sounds nice.

If you've taken basic economics classes, you learned about the rational consumer who carefully weighs something called "utility" (a proxy for enjoyment) that would be received from consuming a widget (a generic consumption good or service). The goal is to maximize total utility by consuming a basket of goods and services. This can get quite complex because there are so many possibilities – how can one obtain the right combo?

You are going to need advanced math to make the right choice, so you'd better study calculus rather than going to the movies! What you want is to ensure that you get the same amount of utility from the very last unit of each one of those consumables you consume. If you know calculus, you are already ahead of the game: you need to equate the *marginal utilities* of each.

There's one more condition: your budget constraint. You are limited in your purchases of consumables by your budget. That, in turn, depends on your income. You must work to get income. Work is not fun. You'd rather go to the movies. So, you'll need a bit more calculus to make the right choice.

You work because you want income so you can buy consumables and maximize utility, subject to your income constraint. But you also want leisure. Work gives you "disutility" (the opposite of pleasure); leisure gives you utility. How much should you work? Up to the point where the marginal disutility of work equals the marginal utility you can obtain from one last dollar of spending on your consumption basket.

Whew! That was a difficult decision! You do this for every single item you purchase, indeed, for every decision you make.

Marriage? Lots of trade-offs. You must calculate the stream of utility you can get for all the possible mates – since polygamy is ruled out in the US (and much of the rest of the world), choice of one eliminates the choice of others. You choose the mate that maximizes your lifetime-worth of utility. Your mate's own utility doesn't concern you, but your mate's earning capacity will be considered. Of course, all of your possible spouses are figuring out the utility they'd get from marrying you, compared against the pleasure they'd get from all their other possible matings. It's amazing that a successful pairing is ever achieved given the complex math involved in decision-making.

There is a lot more to "consumer choice theory" that could be added – including an extended discussion of the nature of "rational man," who is presumed to be solely self-interested (completely unaffected by the happiness, or pain, of others), who has perfect foresight (and no second thoughts about decisions made) – but Thorstein Veblen, the "father" of the institutional approach to economics, famously summed it up in this tongue-firmly-in-cheek way:

The hedonistic conception of man is that of a lightning calculator of pleasures and pains, who oscillates like a homogeneous globule of desire of happiness under the impulse of stimuli that shift him about the area but leave him intact. He has neither antecedent nor consequent. He is an isolated, definitive human datum, in stable equilibrium except for the buffets of the impinging forces that displace him in one direction or another. Self-poised in elemental space, he spins symmetrically about his own spiritual axis until the parallelogram of forces bears down on him, whereupon he follows the line of the resultant.[1]

Consumers are not the only ones facing trade-offs. Investors must choose among alternatives: should I invest in government bonds or corporate bonds? Should I build a new tire factory or get into refrigerator production? Should I hire more workers, or replace them with robots? Or I might decide to hold safe financial assets instead. Such decisions are constrained by budgets; hence, we weigh marginal costs against marginal revenues expected from every possible choice, allocating our spending on investment such that the last dollar spent will generate the maximum feasible profits of the alternatives.

Stripped of the complexity, the math, some extreme assumptions, and the jargon, all of this is perfectly sensible. Of course, we must make choices, and of course we face trade-offs.

But we make lots of mistakes. We choose the movie, we perform poorly on our calculus exam, and we end up in a two-year community college. We choose the wrong spouse, end up divorced, and the divorce court judge awards the house to our former spouse. We often regret the choices we made and would do it all differently if only we had the second chance.

Behavioral psychologists teach that humans are actually

pretty bad at choosing. Choices are not made rationally, but rather are heavily influenced by evolution – which has a long reach across the millions of years it took to produce humanoids. In many situations, we don't behave that much differently than our small-brained ape ancestors. In truth, not that much different from rats. And, surprisingly, the more choices we face, the worse we do – just like rats. As The Clash put it, we get "all lost in the supermarket" – with the clipped coupons and looking for the special offers – unable to make a choice. Best to just grab the first item store management has helpfully placed right at eye level!

Beyond that, there are two problems with the "trade-off" approach to decision-making.

We already touched on one earlier: investments today can relax tomorrow's budget constraints. Studying for your calculus exam can get you higher-paying jobs in the future, which raises your lifetime earnings – pushing that budget constraint out, letting you consume more of everything. The firm that invests in a new factory raises profit potential for the future, meaning more investments later.

Furthermore, the prospect of higher future income makes it possible to access credit – which relieves the budget constraint. In addition to your income, you can borrow and spend beyond today's income. If all turns out as expected, tomorrow's income will be higher, too. Budget constraints are not fixed.

To be sure, this does not completely invalidate the conventional approach to decision-making. You still must allocate spending to maximize utility (consumer) or profit (firm), and making a choice means not taking the alternative. And the decision to invest (in education or factories) is a decision to "postpone" consumption, which is said to depend on the rate of time preference (essentially, thriftiness – save now, consume more later because you can earn interest). That is taken to be different across individuals but largely left unexplained – some peoples are presumed to be naturally more thrifty than others. Saving rates are low in English-speaking nations and high in Asian nations. Maybe there are just no English words to let you say "no" to credit.[2]

The second problem with the approach is more important and is based on the difference between individuals and society as a whole. At the level of the individual it is reasonable to argue that income is the main determinant of spending – with the caveat that today's income can be supplemented by borrowing. Perhaps we do not do too much damage to reality by presuming that individuals face an income constraint – hence, spending faces a trade-off given income.

But at the level of the economy as a whole, spending determines income. At the aggregate level, society can always decide to spend more (it cannot simply decide to have more income). All the spending must end up as income: every dollar spent gets received by someone. This is the way that our national accounting is set up: total spending (GDP) equals total income (gross national income, GNI).

Our budget "constraint" is determined by our spending – not the other way around. If we spend more, the income "constraint" is larger. For the nation as a whole.

But how can we as a nation spend more than our income? Well, we cannot, because whatever we spend becomes our income! But we can spend more than last year's income – which makes this year's income greater than last year's. That is how GDP and GNI grow every year – outside recessions and depressions. And government spends more, too, increasing income. The general trend is always up because each year we decide to spend more and that increases our income.

How can we keep doing this year after year? The key, of course, is credit. Private financial institutions create money to finance spending, and government creates money to finance its spending. Together that creates income. And growing income allows us to make the payments on the debts from the past.

Trying to extrapolate from individual behavior and constraints to the aggregate almost always leads to the wrong conclusion. It is such a common mistake that we have a name for it: fallacy of composition. And, indeed, a whole branch of economics – called "macroeconomics" – is devoted to trying to correct the errors.

What is true at the individual level is almost never true at the aggregate. The reverse is also valid: what is true at the aggregate is almost never true at the individual level.

If *you* continually tried to spend more than your income, you probably would find that your income wouldn't increase (at least, not sufficiently), and you'd end up in the poorhouse. But if we – all of us – try to spend more than our income, we – at the national level – would find our income higher!

It is thus wrong to think that if at the aggregate level we spend more on one thing, then we must spend less on something else. That's just not correct. We can spend more on both.

B. Public Trade-Offs

This brings us to public trade-offs. We hear politicians saying all the time: if I ran my household budget the way that Uncle Sam runs his, I'd go bankrupt. Uncle Sam has spent more than his tax revenue in about 80 percent of the years since the nation was founded almost 250 years ago. His debt-to-GDP ratio has grown at a rate of 1.8 percent since the founding – owing $28 trillion as of 2021. If I owed that much, I'd be in big trouble!

But where's the trade-off?

In our first economics course, we are taught that the economy faces a trade-off: guns or butter? If we spend more on the military (guns), we have got to spend less on our population's consumption (butter). This is the public (guns) and private (butter) trade-off. More government spending means less private spending.

And in the more advanced public finance course, we learn the government's equivalent of the utility maximization problem: we need to weigh the "marginal social benefit" of government spending against the "marginal social cost," spending up to the point where the last dollar equates the two.

The usual presumption is that without government use, the private sector would tend to operate at full employment of all resources (labor, natural resources, and capital). Hence, public use can only come at the expense of the private sector. Let's examine that claim in some detail.

It is often claimed that government spending by its very nature is "inefficient," and even that it is not "productive." If that were true, then taking resources from private sector use and using them in the public sector would reduce the nation's productive capacity. Hence, not only is there a trade-off, but the size of the "economic pie" might even be reduced if resources are moved to the public sector.

This is an extreme view that ignores the important role played by government in providing public infrastructure (roads, airports), education and training, a system of rules, laws, and regulation, and public health measures (water and sewage treatment – which have probably done more to improve health and increase life spans than any medical advances). Further, going forward it is difficult to see how the private sector plausibly could be expected to deal with the multiple challenges created by global pandemics and impending climate catastrophe.

We'll examine policy issues later, but here will take it for granted that at least some public spending does enhance productive capacity. Further, as we pointed out earlier, there isn't strong evidence that bigger government reduces economic growth – most rich countries have relatively bigger governments than the US has, without obvious performance problems.

To the extent that government spending on things like public physical and human infrastructure development (what we called the capital development of the economy in chapter 3), the view of a trade-off must be modified. Even if we must move resources from the private sector, meaning less private production now, we can have more resources in the future for both the private and the public sector to use. Much like private investment, government spending can raise living standards – by relaxing the resource constraints. We can have more guns *and* more butter.

Moreover, the presumption that the private sector has a strong tendency to move the economy toward full employment of all resources is belied by the evidence. In the US before the 1930s, the federal government was very small (except in major wars like the Civil War and World War I) – indeed, its spending was only about 3 percent of GDP on the eve of the Great Depression. Did that small government leave room for the private sector to operate near to full employment most of the time?

No. The economy cycled between expansion and deep depression approximately once each generation. Most Americans know of the Great Depression of the 1930s, but they do not know that was our sixth depression. And they are not fully aware of the association of the growth of the federal government from 3 percent in 1929 to an average of about 25 percent after World War II with the complete absence of depressions since the "Great" one. Further, the period following the Great Depression and the rise of Big Government in the US has been called the "golden era" of US capitalism and made up most of the second half of the century that economist Robert Gordon calls the "special century," with productivity growth three times greater than the half-century that preceded it.[3]

The important point is that in spite of strong beliefs that "free markets" generate full employment, neither rigorous theory nor historical experience shows that to be true. The typical case is that our economy operates with substantial amounts of labor and capital resources that are underutilized. There is a positive role for the government to play in mobilizing unemployed resources. (We'll return to that in sections D and F of this chapter and again in chapter 7.)

As we've mentioned, the conventional view is that government can supplement taxes with borrowing (selling government bonds) or money printing (an option not available to households or firms). The government's budget constraint is thus somewhat less restricted by income (its tax revenue) – therefore, conventional thinking is that both borrowing and money printing should be carefully limited, with government spending constrained to spending tax revenue. MMT rejects that framework, arguing that all government spending always takes the form of keystroke money credits. We won't explore that in more detail now but will continue to focus on the supposed constraints involved in government spending.

Regarding the income constraint, the situation of the national government is very different from that of the firm or household. The national income is the government's "oyster,"[4] in the sense that total tax revenue is related to total national income. Since, as we saw in the previous section, spending determines income, government spending goes into determining national income. A household's personal consumption spending is a drop in the national bucket of income and is not likely to raise that household's income by even a penny. Government's spending is a significant share of total spending (a quarter to a half of all spending, depending on the country) – so large that it will affect government's income (tax revenue).

Further – and here's an important concept that you may have learned in your basic macroeconomics course – government's spending raises private income, which is likely to raise private spending. This is called the "multiplier effect" – the private spending induced by government spending. That extra private spending also raises national income. And that, too, raises government tax revenue.

Precisely how much national income and government revenues will rise when government spends depends on many factors and the state of the economy – and is highly contested. But good economic performance – which government spending can help maintain – significantly raises tax revenue.

More importantly, as we've discussed, government typically spends an amount greater than tax revenue – incurring deficits. Government's deficits are our surpluses. They create income that we can save, spend, or use to repay our own debts. Uncle Sam's $28 trillion debt (as of 2021) means that "we" (everyone who is not Uncle Sam, all taken together) have $28 trillion of financial wealth. Unlike a household, a sovereign government never needs to repay any of its debt. Uncle Sam only repaid his debt one time – back in 1837 under President Jackson. Our first depression followed that. Uncle Sam is not likely to ever do it again. Instead of repaying the debt, he rolls it over into new debt.

Why does a household have to repay debt – either during life or at death? Because death is one of the two certainties in life (the other is taxes). It surprises people to learn that banks aren't that crazy about you repaying your loans *before* death. So long as you remain creditworthy and can pay the interest, banks would, in principle, be perfectly happy to continually roll over your loan into a new loan. Keep you on the hook forever – paying interest to the bank. We even have loans like that – called "interest-only" loans. For many people, the standard thirty-year fixed rate mortgage loan is effectively a "forever" loan in the sense that they will either die or sell the house before they actually pay off the loan. However, when they do sell the house, or die, the loan must be repaid. The bank cannot squeeze interest payments out of a corpse.

In principle, the sovereign government has an infinite life span. Now, we know that no government has – yet – lasted forever; and probably none ever will. However, we do not contemplate the end of our government – we put that to the back of our minds and act as if Uncle Sam will last forever. And that he'll make those interest payments forever. And, hence, there's no reason not to let him roll over the debt. Forever.

Besides, if our government comes to an end, interest payments on Uncle Sam's bonds will probably be the least of our worries. We'll have bigger fish to fry.

C. Is Policy a Zero-Sum Game?

A lot of conventional economic theory presumes that policy is a zero-sum game: there must be a winner and a loser. If the state of West Virginia gets some "pork" from Congress, there must be losses in some other state. There are lots of different arguments used to lead to this conclusion. Some are based on a flawed view of government finance. Some are based on a flawed view of resources. And some are based on a dog-eat-dog, Hobbesian view of the "realpolitik" nature of policy. While there might be some truth in the last of these, it need not be so.

Two of the most ubiquitous claims attributed to economics are: (1) resources are scarce but wants are unlimited; and (2) there's no such thing as a free lunch.

The first leads to what is called "the economic problem," which also happens to be the most popular title of the second chapter of economics textbooks. What happens when unlimited wants come up against resources that are scarce? Well, as The Rolling Stones put it, "You can't always get what you want." Above we outlined conventional consumer theory, with its utility maximization. Although the marginal utility you get from adding units of a particular good tends to decline (ultimately to zero), you are presumed never to be fully satiated across all possible consumption goods and services.

Think of beer. After the third or fourth, you enjoy each next beer less and less. By the sixth – or perhaps tenth, depending on your "preferences" – you've had enough. You move on to pretzels. And so on. But you never reach a point where you'd decline *something*. How about a Tesla?[5]

Add up those unlimited wants across the global population of 8 billion people and you've got a humongous demand. And by assumption, no matter how much stuff is supplied, they'd still want more. They can never be fully satiated.

But resources are scarce, by assumption. It turns out this is a critical assumption. Only scarce resources have a price that allocates them according to the laws of supply and demand. Resources that are not scarce have a zero price and hence cannot be marketed. So, whether or not resources really *are* scarce, conventional economics requires them to be so – otherwise conventional economics cannot analyze them. There's no economic problem unless resources are scarce but wants are not.

The free market then puts a price on the scarce resources, and willingness (and ability) to pay allocates them efficiently. They all get used. This is why there's no free lunch. All resources must be presumed to be fully utilized, so trying to provide more resources to someone must create a loss to someone else. Economics is called "the dismal science." There's no such thing as a free lunch. That's dismal.

If policy makers come along with a plan to shift some of those resources, there must be winners (who get more than they had) and losers (who end up with less than they had). For example, government decides to play the role of Robin Hood, taking from the rich and giving to the poor. The poor win; the rich lose. Is there some way to determine whether the net effect is positive – can a Robin Hood policy benefit the winners more than it hurts the losers?

Well, we cannot say with certainty. The poor get more "utils" and the rich lose some "utils." Utils are the units of utility you get – the satisfaction you get from consuming widgets. Unfortunately, the experts tell us there is no way to measure them "cardinally" – we cannot put a number on it – and there's no way to compare utils across the rich and poor.

Who are we to say that the rich get less satisfaction from spending one more dollar on consumption than the poor get from a dollar? That dollar might buy the rich guy one additional drop of a nice wine to go with dinner, or the poor guy a cup of rice to stave off starvation. Who knows which guy is enjoying that dollar the most? Certainly not a conventional economist.[6] This makes picking winners and losers a fraught business. That rice lunch is not free.

Much of the argument made to demonstrate that policy is a zero-sum game is centered on the finance of government spending. If government "pays for" its spending by taxing, the taxpayer is the loser – taxes make the taxpayer's budget constraint tighter. However, there is something called a "balanced budget multiplier" that proves a $100 tax to "pay for" government spending of $100 will still lead to a net increase of national income and spending. We won't go through the mathematical proof here, but the reasoning is that if you must pay $100 in taxes, you will "pay for" that by reducing both consumption and saving. If you typically would have saved $10 out of each $100 of income, then you will reduce consumption by $90 and saving by $10 to come up with the $100 to pay the tax. Hence, by analogy if everyone else does the same thing, for every $100 of government spending, consumption falls by $90 so we end up with a "balanced budget" increase of national spending of $10 (for each $100 of spending and taxing as consumption falls by only $10). The government spending is not "zero-sum" because there is some increase of the total spending. Still, there is a "cost" because consumption fell by $90.

What if government instead borrowed to "pay for" the spending? There's no tax increase, so it seems like $100 of spending would increase national spending and income by $100. But if we presume that finance, itself, is a scarce resource, then the government's demand for that will "crowd out" private borrowing. The "price" of credit is the interest rate. As the government increases its demand for finance, the interest rate supposedly rises; as it rises, private sector borrowers decide to reduce their borrowing (because they don't want to pay the higher rate). We get more government borrowing and less private borrowing, and more government spending and less private spending. That's crowding out.

How much crowding out is there? There's a huge debate among conventional economists about this – some think it is small because private spending is not very interest-sensitive; others think it is big. There are various approaches to this but to cut a long story short, in some of the approaches crowding out could be complete, or even more than complete. If it is complete, then $100 of government borrowing reduces private borrowing and spending by $100; if more than complete, private borrowing and spending fall by more than $100 – and we end up with lower national income than we had before the government borrowed. In that case, government spending financed with a deficit would be zero-sum (or even worse than zero-sum): government wins, private borrowers lose.

What about just printing money to pay for the spending? For most conventional economists, that would be too dangerous to even consider; for a few it might be OK, but only in an emergency (such as a global health pandemic!). If government attempted it, the result would be inflation, according to many conventional economists. Since inflation would reduce the purchasing power of money, the government would have to print more money to pay the higher prices. That would cause inflation to spiral and prompt even more money-printing. This is the usual explanation of hyperinflation – government causes it by printing money. Soon we are off to Zimbabwean levels of hyperinflation. For that reason, this is not seen as a plausible option – it doesn't really move resources to the government because the purchasing power of the government's currency falls in proportion to the amount of currency it issues. It is the path to rack and ruin of the economy.

D. What is MMT's View on All This?

First, MMT (like many heterodox approaches to economics) rejects the assumption that resources are scarce. Resources are created by human effort. While it is certainly true that the "gifts of nature" are not exhaustible – indeed, they are in grave danger – the resources we need to satisfy our needs are mostly produced by humans. Production processes do rely on natural resources, and we must learn how to use them in a sustainable manner. But the most important resource is human labor – broadly defined to include the imagination and innovation that our big brains are made for.

Those labor resources are rarely – if ever – fully utilized and are capable of expansion. In part through population growth (and inclusion of a higher percent of the population in the labor force), but mostly through expansion of human capabilities – through education, training, and inclusive treatment of humans of all types. Elimination of discriminatory practices and marginalization of populations (women, people of color, people with disabilities, aged people, people in the global south, and the LGBTQIA community) will also greatly expand our labor resources.

Operating closer to full employment will also encourage investment in robot technology – to replace human labor. While this is generally feared when unemployment is widespread, if we operated our economy at continuous full employment, it would be welcomed as a supplement to human labor. Let the robots do the dreary work. Exactly what they will do while leaving the rest to humans is a policy choice.

MMT, like other heterodox approaches, also rejects the assumption that wants are naturally insatiable. Wants are socially produced – and there is nothing natural about wanting an infinite amount of stuff. Further, many wants, by their very nature, are for what we call public goods – goods that private markets cannot supply in sufficient quantities. One of the characteristics of public goods is that they can be "nonrival" in consumption. What this means is that my use of them does not interfere with your use. In many cases this is a matter of degree: a public park can be enjoyed by many people – although it could become too crowded, at which point it becomes "rival." An outdoor concert is similarly nonrival, up to a point. Once broadband is in place, a lot of consumption over the internet is essentially nonrival – we can all enjoy an online talk by, say, Noam Chomsky! And a publicly supplied internet could be free – a publicly supplied public good.

In any event, we – society – have some input to determine the nature of wants. We have so far largely left this up to private advertising – which, predictably, has manufactured wants centered on what for-profit producers want us to buy. Advertising for cigarettes manufactured a "want" to become addicted to a dangerous substance that has killed hundreds of millions of humans. After many decades of deaths piling up, we changed our collective minds. There was nothing "natural" about this "want" or the early deaths it produced.

Second, MMT rejects the notion that government *chooses* to tax, borrow, or print money. All government spending takes the same form: keystroke credits to bank reserves. We can choose to leave those in the banks or can sell bonds. This is not a borrowing operation. It does not crowd out any private borrowing, even if we do sell the bonds. Bond sales offer interest, they do not bid up interest rates. Indeed, all else equal, if government spends without selling bonds, its "deficit" pushes interest rates down (not up) to the central bank's floor rate (what it pays on reserves). Interest rates on reserves and on short-maturity bonds are directly set by central bank policy; and those short-term rates largely determine the rates even on long-term government bonds. If rates rise, it is the central bank that raises them – not "markets."

Third, taxes serve several purposes – as will be discussed in more detail in chapter 6. One of the purposes is to reduce private sector net (after tax) income in order to reduce private spending. Hence, MMT does accept the conventional claim that the taxpayer "loses." That is a feature, not a bug, of the tax system. A major purpose of taxes is to free up resources by reducing net private income and spending – and once resources are freed by taxes, the government can move them to the public purpose. That is a legitimate purpose of taxes. In other words, taxes can be used to create policy space for government spending. This is how government avoids inflation as it increases spending.

However, to be clear, we do not need to create policy space through taxes if there already are unemployed resources the government can tap. At full employment, imposing more taxes to reduce private use of resources leaves space for government spending without having to bid the resources away with higher price offers. But even in that case, it would not be correct to jump to the conclusion that the government's spending is zero-sum. If taxes reduce private spending that is offset by government spending, society as a whole can still gain – if government spending enhances public welfare. MMT concedes that it is sometimes difficult to determine whether the losses to the private sector are more than made up for by social gains due to government spending.

This leads us to the final consideration: politics.

When it comes to government spending, three questions rise to the surface: can government spend more? Should government spend more? And, if so, what should government spend more *on*?

MMT provides a clear answer to the first question: yes, government can spend more. Keystrokes – you cannot run out of them. To the second question, MMT answers that if there are unemployed resources, government ought to spend more. To the third question, MMT has a partial answer: jobs. Government ought to create more jobs for the unemployed. We have some tentative ideas on what kinds of jobs. By focusing on jobs, MMT does not want to imply that government shouldn't spend more on anything but creating jobs. But MMT does prioritize jobs: involuntary unemployment is extremely costly, both for the individuals who are unemployed and also for society as a whole. In chapter 7, we will discuss MMT's approach to ensuring full employment through a job guarantee program.

MMT proponents have their own preferences regarding what else government ought to do – some might want

Medicare-For-All; others might want Green New Deal spending; some want more paid family leave; and so on. MMT, by itself, doesn't lead to any particular position on these policies – it just makes it clear that we can financially afford them. Do we have the resources to successfully undertake them? Not necessarily – we might need to free up some resource to make policy space for those proposals. Do we have the necessary political support to push them through Congress? Who knows? The policy agenda is better left to the political arena, with input from researchers.

Many will find this less than satisfactory. Some don't trust politicians. Some don't trust democracy. Some don't trust the "experts" who will produce the analyses that will influence the politicians. Most are probably skeptical of the lobbyists who will try to influence the outcome. Many Americans have given up hope in the democratic process and staked their hopes in a former reality TV star who fashions himself to be the next dictator, imposing his own twisted preferences on society.

Policy making cannot be separated from politics. We've chosen democracy in the hope that the politics will (eventually) lead to policy that serves the public interest. But, as Ringo Starr said, "It don't come easy."

E. Why We Should Take Advantage of the Free Lunches

Let us conclude with a call for taking our free lunches where we can find them. As mentioned, economics is known for arguing that there's no such thing as a free lunch. That is preposterous. Free lunches abound – it is a policy failure to refuse to take advantage of them. If there are unemployed resources, it is possible to put them to use in a manner that gives us a free lunch. And taking those free lunches can pay off in multiples if we use them wisely to build capacity.

Hiring an unemployed worker is a free lunch. If we take the view that all humans have rights to access some basic necessities, we must support someone whether she works or not. Even if her contributions to the social welfare are relatively small, if they increase by employing her, society wins. It is a free lunch. We must be careful in our calculation, however, as we need to consider her unpaid contributions before she got employment. If she was caring for family members while unemployed, and if her pay on the job is too low to hire a substitute to care for the family, then the net benefit from employing her could be zero or negative. In that case, it is not a free lunch. Adequate pay as well as benefits (including childcare) are necessary to ensure we can enjoy the free lunches.

And sometimes it makes sense to pay for lunches that are not free – if they are socially desirable. Hiring people with severe disabilities may not net much output, but it is important to find space for anyone who wants to participate and contribute.

As discussed above, using resources to expand capacity means not only that we enjoy more employment and income and output today, but also that we can have even more in the future. If we put unemployed resources to work, we need to ensure that at least some of those are used to increase capacity – both private and public "infrastructure" broadly defined to include both physical and human capacity.

Among economists there is something known as "Okun's Law," which is a rule of thumb based on empirical data – not really some law of economics or nature. Professor Okun had studied the data and estimated that each one-percentage-point drop of the official unemployment rate increases GDP by three percentage points. This may not seem like a lot, but a growth of GDP by 3 percent is a really big deal – over $700 billion worth of additional output in 2021. In an economic boom, GDP might grow by 6 percent in a year. Dropping the official unemployment rate from 5 percent to 3 percent would give us the

6 percent growth of a boom. To be sure, this is a one-time boost; to continue it in the second year we would have to go from 3 percent to 1 percent to give us an additional 6 percent of GDP – difficult but perhaps not impossible. But we quickly run out of room to continue to lower the rate through unemployment rate reductions.

However, the point is that we've experienced chronically high unemployment for decades – giving up output each year equal to several times 3 percent of GDP according to Okun's Law. Those were potential free lunches. And bypassing them meant that we did not use them to increase capacity. Further, private firms were not incentivized to increase capacity because slower growth and higher unemployment reduced the impetus to invest. If labor is cheap and easily available, firms don't invest in labor-productivity-enhancing capital. If consumption is growing slowly, they don't increase capacity. If we don't take advantage of free lunches, we not only suffer less employment, income, and output now, but we reduce our ability to produce in the future below what it might have been.

The output lost over decades of relatively high unemployment is so large we have trouble contemplating it. If we had taken advantage of all those free lunches, we could have made a huge dent in world poverty. That we didn't is in large measure the fault of economists spreading the falsehood that "there's no such thing as a free lunch." It is a stain on the profession, perhaps the biggest of all economic lies.

F. The Inflation–Unemployment Trade-off

Earlier we have briefly addressed the issue of inflation. Many fear that there is a trade-off: if government spends more to try to reduce unemployment, this will cause inflation. There's no free lunch involved when it comes to creating jobs – the cost is inflation. Let's examine the argument. To be clear, however, if more jobs leads to inflation, this should be true of private spending, too. If the "cost" of reducing unemployment is inflation, we should also worry about private employers hiring workers. We should fear announcements by a big company like Amazon that it plans to increase hiring. In practice, those announcements are generally cheered, but, paradoxically, more employment by government as well as falling unemployment rates are feared as harbingers of inflation.

In chapter 7, we will look at MMT's proposal for full employment, but let's examine the evolution of thinking about the unemployment–inflation trade-off.

In the early 1960s many economists believed in a simple policy trade-off: government could spend to raise aggregate demand to reduce unemployment. However, this would increase the rate of inflation. Lowering inflation by cutting spending would cause unemployment to increase. The preferences of policy makers would determine the "sweet spot" – the preferred combination of inflation and unemployment. The Democrat party would choose, say, inflation of 4 percent and unemployment of 3 percent; the Republican party would prefer inflation of 2 percent and unemployment of 5 percent. The trade-off was presumed to be relatively stable, so where we ended up would simply reflect the preferences of the party in power. Economists gave the trade-off a name: the Phillips Curve. It was accepted as something like an economic law.

This generated a revolution of thought among economists. The experience of the Great Depression had led economists to believe that unemployment is an evil that ought to be fought by policy makers. The Roosevelt administration had created a New Deal that included a variety of employment programs for the unemployed. After World War II, Congress passed the Employment Act of 1946, committing policy makers to pursuit of low unemployment – which would be fought as an economic disease by keeping aggregate spending high. But the rise of the notion of a Phillips Curve trade-off led to a change of thinking. Unemployment was not a disease but rather a policy solution: we need unemployed workers to keep inflation at bay. If there is an insufficient supply of the unemployed to keep wages down, wages and prices would rise.[7]

This seemed to fit the US data in the 1960s. However, the relationship between unemployment and inflation fell apart in the early 1970s – both inflation and unemployment rose: rather than a trade-off, we got rising inflation with rising unemployment – called stagflation. Later, after the mid-1980s, we got falling inflation with falling unemployment. And since 1990, unemployment has risen and fallen without demonstrating any sort of a trade-off with inflation. There is no negative, stable relation between inflation and unemployment that can be found in the data.

Still, the view that unemployment is a tool that policy makers should use to fight inflation had become ingrained by the late 1960s. The Fed, especially, continued to use a falling unemployment rate as an excuse to tighten monetary policy through the 1980s, 1990s, and even into the 2000s – in the absence of evidence for a Phillips Curve trade-off. Only very gradually did the dogma come into question. Since the GFC, however, economists and some researchers at the Fed have argued that the so-called Phillips Curve trade-off is not supported by the data, and as a result the Fed has been more hesitant about raising interest rates when unemployment rates come down – for the simple reason that lower unemployment has not led to higher inflation.

The MMT view is that high aggregate demand – whether resulting from government spending or from private spending – *can* lead to rising wages and prices. The official measure of the unemployment rate is not a very accurate guide, however, because it misses a very large portion of those without jobs (or with part-time jobs) who would be willing to work full-time if jobs were offered. They don't get counted among the unemployed for a variety of reasons, including because they have worked a few hours during the survey week, or because they did not actively seek a job. This is one of the reasons that low measured unemployment doesn't generate inflation – there are plenty of uncounted workers ready and willing to work.

Further, MMT argues that many factors go into determining whether low unemployment will lead to rising wages and prices. For example, if domestic labor has to compete with cheap foreign labor, it is difficult to press for wage increases – even if the unemployment rate is low. American firms can close up factories in the US and expand production abroad rather than paying higher wages. Similarly, American firms do not have much pricing power if they compete with foreign firms – hence, high demand does not lead to price increases. Finally, rising productivity can lower production costs and offset pressures on prices coming from high aggregate demand.

MMT argues that much of the experience with higher inflation in the 1970s was not really due to high aggregate demand, but rather was produced by high costs on the supply side. For example, there were two "oil price shocks" – one in the early 1970s and another at the end of that decade – when OPEC greatly increased the price of oil. Since oil is an input to most production processes and a component of the consumer basket, it was not a surprise that prices, in general, would rise. As prices rose, workers tried to catch up by demanding higher wages. Since the problem was not really one of excess aggregate demand, it was a mistake to fight this supply-side-induced inflation by adopting austerity policy. That only increased unemployment without resolving any of the issues that caused prices to rise – so we got the twin evils of stagflation. Note that explains why both inflation and unemployment rose – the opposite of the Phillips Curve trade-off.

In 2021 the US experienced a similar situation: problems on the supply side led to increased costs and rising prices. These problems were largely created by the global COVID-19 pandemic, which disrupted production and supply chains. OPEC also took advantage of the situation by reducing output and raising prices. Many workers were forced to leave their jobs due to health precautions, and then were reluctant to return either out of fear for their safety or due to obligations to care for family members. So, again, we had prices rising while unemployment (measured and unmeasured) was high. Many factors went into creating price pressures – it was not a simple matter of "too much spending." This time, policy makers were wisely reluctant to adopt austerity, and the Fed showed patience in holding off interest rate hikes.

At the same time, the administration of President Biden was pushing for an ambitious "Build Back Better" program that would ramp up spending over the decade of the 2020s. Many feared the program was too big – all the spending was said to be sure to cause inflation. MMT argues that we need to focus our attention on the resources that will be needed, not on the program's cost in terms of dollars – no matter how many trillions would be spent. We agree that if the program is not carefully phased in at a pace that is consistent with our capacity to mobilize the resources needed, there could be inflationary consequences. There could well be a trade-off: we may need to release resources from private use so that we can use them in Biden's program. But that is not a foregone conclusion and inflation can be avoided through careful implementation of the program.

To sum up, MMT agrees that when aggregate demand is high enough to push up against productive capacity, this could pressure prices. At what point this would cause sustained inflation, and how high the inflation might be, depend on a variety of factors, including degree of competition from abroad, strength of labor unions, degree of monopolization of the domestic economy (and collusion among producers to raise prices), and so on.

There are two important points to be made: there is nothing special about government spending – private spending could also push demand up against productive capacity; and we have rarely, if ever, faced such a situation except during major wars (such as World War II). Finally, even if we were to face sustainable inflation, raising unemployment to fight it is not necessarily the best strategy.

6
The MMT Alternative Framework for Policy

A. Framing

On one level MMT is descriptive. It provides a correct description of the operation of a sovereign currency system. It is necessary to understand money to put it to use in service of the public interest. Science is necessarily a progressive endeavor – we use science to solve problems and to better the human condition. Or, as American comedian Stephen Colbert put it at the White House Correspondents' Dinner for President George W. Bush, reality has a well-known liberal bias. Of course it does.

From global warming to the problems of unemployment, the progressive perspective is based on reality, while the conservative view necessarily denies science. However, we do not want to make the mistake of presuming that knowledge alone will ensure politicians do what is right. To win the policy debates, we must win the moral argument that policy should serve the public interest.

In recent years, MMT has been launched into the limelight, but it still faces huge barriers. Money is a difficult topic – even for those who want to understand it. While it would be nice if we could distil MMT down to a single nice catchphrase, I do not think that is possible. Money is hard stuff. It is contentious. To be sure, the conventional story is wrong – it is inconsistent with the findings of historians, anthropologists, legal scholars, sociologists, and political scientists.[1] No part of the conservative story of money has been verified by scholars working in these disciplines. The MMT view presented in the chapters above is more consistent with these findings. But it is not enough to explain what money is and how it works. Because *how* we frame our arguments is important.

This chapter explores MMT's alternative framework for analyzing the sovereign's money. Virtually everything written about money in economics textbooks, in policy think-tank documents, and by the media reflects what linguist George Lakoff calls a conservative framework.[2] Even expositions by progressive economists predominantly use the conservative framework.

Lakoff emphasizes that all words are defined relative to frames. Progressives usually adopt words used by conservatives, which evoke the conservative frames. Once evoked, the conservative frames cannot be overcome. Even worse, progressives typically begin an argument with reference to the conservative view, then attempt to destroy it through argument. This is a strategy that is sure to fail. Lakoff explains why, using the following example.

Don't think of an elephant! Do not imagine its long, snaking trunk. The ridiculously thin and short tail worthy of a mouse. The legs as sturdy as trees. The huge feet and tusks. And whatever you do, don't think of big floppy ears that if rapidly flapped might lift the elephant for a flight.

OK. Are you thinking of Dumbo? Of course you are. You cannot get that elephant out of your head. You will be thinking about him for the rest of the day.

We need an alternative framework, one that provides a frame that is consistent with a progressive social view. And to deal with all the challenges facing our nation. It cannot begin from markets, from free exchange, from individual choice. We need a social metaphor, a public interest alternative to the private maximization calculus. We need to focus on the positive role played by government, and its use of money to serve us well.

We also know from experience that "truth" doesn't automatically trump myth. George Lakoff has brilliantly explained how our minds work, using metaphors – little stories – to understand the world. This is especially true the more abstract the concept under examination. Economics uses highly abstract concepts and reasoning: "economy," "market," "equilibrium," "productivity," "supply and demand," and, especially, "money." None of these concepts has a concrete real-world counterpart. All are abstract concepts that rely on metaphors to develop understanding.

MMT is as correct as a theory can be, and as good a description as we have about real-world monetary operations. None of the critics has been able to provide a credible refutation of any of the principles of MMT. The reaction against MMT is not based on theory. It is not based on empirical evidence. It is not fact-based.

It is moral.

That is not a backhanded slap at critics. You cannot understand without metaphors; you cannot think without stories; you cannot do policy analysis without morality.

Outside of the crazies, everyone knows the US government cannot run out of money – which is one of the main themes of this book. The truth is simple: Uncle Sam *cannot* be forced into insolvency.

No matter how many times a pundit declares that the federal government is spending its way to the poorhouse, all educated economists, policy makers, and politicians know that *it just ain't true*. And so the way that an MMT-er approaches pervasive deficit hysteria is by pointing out that as the federal government spends through keystrokes that credit bank accounts, it can afford anything for sale in US dollars.

The reaction typically goes through four stages: incredulity, fear, moral indignation, and anger. Rather than winning the debate about how money "works," MMT loses the argument. How can that be?

Because people believe it is *immoral* for the government to spend through the stroke of a key.

It makes no difference how accurately MMT explains the monetary operations, it will lose the argument by precisely presenting the facts, because one can see facts only through framing. Without the proper framing, MMT cannot win policy debates.

In this chapter we explain how to use the MMT framing to promote understanding and policies consistent with MMT. We won't go deeply into the details of Lakoff's theories, but we will use his teachings to provide a framework consistent with the findings of MMT.

B. MMT's Framework on Money

Let's see how MMT should approach the framing to many of the topics surrounding money that we have addressed.

We can think of "memes" that are planted in the subconscious of everyone – they are little stories that we use to organize our thoughts. We all learn stories and the lessons from these can be triggered by terms and phrases. They are sort of like viruses that lay in wait. And, like viruses, they spread from brain to brain. Conservatives understand this and use it to their advantage. We must learn how to use them to our advantage.

I think Bruce Springsteen has got the starting point for our policy goal: We take care of our own. We is all of us. Our own is all of us. We are all of us in this together.

- *We take care of our own.*[3]

That is our opening gambit.

Policy is always and everywhere a moral issue – not merely an economic issue and certainly not merely a technical issue. To win policy debates, we must – like orthodoxy

– engage the moral issues. We can take the higher moral ground. To do so, we need to develop an MMT alternative for our understanding of money – a story of money's origins, nature, functions, and operations.

To that end, we begin with the state and its money, that is, with the state and its treasury and central bank at the center of our monetary system. On one level, that monetary system is a set of credits and debits: I Owe You's and You Owe Me's.

- *One of our themes is: "money is what we owe each other"; or: "money is the tie that binds."*

These IOUs are recorded on balance sheets, with banks handling much of the record-keeping. At the aggregate level, all the IOUs must cancel – there are always two entries, a debit on one account and a credit on another – but that takes away all the fun, all the action. The credits and debits necessarily represent a social relation – the creditor and debtor are related in a social bond.

While we normally think it is better to be a creditor than a debtor, throughout history both parties have always been thought to be tainted by this relationship. As Shakespeare put it: "Neither a borrower nor a lender be." In any case, debt is unavoidable in a society in which much of the economy is organized through and oriented toward the monetary system – which itself consists of layer upon layer of debits and credits.

We've already mentioned the state's choice of the monetary unit. It is difficult to perceive how the haggling of a number of self-interested individuals bartering a reasonably large number of items could ever settle on a single measuring unit. In any case, it is rather clear that today, at least, it really is the state that chooses the money unit (pound, dollar, yen), taxes in the unit, and issues the currency denominated in that unit (again, we recognize the caveat that there are a few minor exceptions, plus one major exception in which EMU (Economic and Monetary Union) member states chose to adopt a common unit and chose to constrain currency issue through self-imposed rules).

C. The MMT View of Taxes

MMT's alternative framework says that "taxes drive money." Let's develop that further.

From the alternative MMT view, the monetary system is a state money system. And from that framing, the most important purpose of taxes is to create a demand for the state's currency. Further, the state really does not need tax revenue to spend and in fact really cannot spend tax revenue. Then why do we need taxes?

- *Our MMT view: taxes create a demand for the currency, ensuring willing sellers of goods and services for money.*

While taxes are largely an involuntary liability, sales to government are largely voluntary. Exactly what one does to obtain the means of paying taxes ("money," although technically taxes are paid using central bank reserves, with payment handled by private banks) is at least in part discretionary. But, as they say, only death and taxes are unavoidable. Most people have to sell something to get the means of paying taxes.

Taxes serve two other important purposes, too. They help to regulate demand – by increasing costs and reducing net income. This is especially important as the economy reaches full employment: if the government continues to increase its resource intake it will drive up prices unless it reduces nongovernment use of resources. Taxes reduce private spending, reducing competition between the government's desire to use resources and private use. That fights inflation.

- *Our meme: taxes help keep the currency strong.*

In addition, sin taxes are used to reduce socially undesirable behavior (and tax credits are used to reward good behavior) by raising the cost of "sin." High tobacco taxes have proven useful in discouraging smoking, especially among young people who are income constrained (and not yet addicted). Another use of taxes is to prevent accumulation of excessive wealth over generations. Tax deductions for charitable giving can drive socially useful contributions. We see that in addition to driving money, taxes can be used to further the public purpose – fighting sin, reducing unearned inheritances, and boosting charitable contributions.

- *Our meme: taxes can help fight sin and reward charity.*

D. MMT's Approach to Spending

At the level of the national government, "taxes don't pay for nothin'." Instead, they serve three purposes: they drive money, they prevent excess demand, and they influence choice. All of these are within the proper purview of public policy; all have substantial social benefits. We need to stress these and discard the conservative tax meme that taxes pay for government.

Now, at the local and state (or provincial) level, government is a "user" of the currency, not an issuer. It needs an income, including tax revenue, bond sales, and federal government "transfers" (or "block grants"). That is true. The federal government can never run out. It should step up to the plate – especially when it comes to social spending – helping state and local governments finance their spending.

- *Our meme: the sovereign government can always afford socially desirable programs. A government that issues its own currency can never run out of keystrokes.*

But affordability is not enough. The only way to win arguments for particular progressive policies is to emphasize sounder moral grounds. We formulate framing consistent with our superior morality.

As mentioned, Bruce Springsteen knows something about framing progressive policy:

> We take care of our own,
> We take care of our own,
> Wherever this flag's flown,
> We take care of our own.

Here's the alternative take on the social safety net:

- *We don't let old folks sleep on the street. We take care of our own.*
- *We don't let children go hungry. We take care of our own.*
- *We're all stakeholders in this great nation. We take care of our own. White, black, brown, we take care of our own. Young or old, healthy or sick, we take care of our own. Male, female, lesbian, straight, gay, queer, bi, and trans, we take care of our own.*

Here's the MMT view on taxes and government spending:

- *We pay taxes to keep our currency strong. A strong currency keeps our country strong. A strong currency and a strong country ensure that we can take care of our own.*
- *We need a good government to help us take care of our own. We need good public services and infrastructure to keep our country strong so that we can take care of our own. Our government spends to keep our country strong so that we can take care of our own.*

Government's authority to spend its currency is baked into the Constitution – which gives to Congress the sole power to issue currency. The amount government is allowed to spend is determined each year through Congressional appropriations. What constrains government spending is neither its tax revenue nor the amount of loose change it can find in sofa cushions. If government is not spending enough, that is the fault of Congress.

• *Our government can always afford to take care of its own.*

Anything that is technologically feasible is financially affordable for the sovereign issuer of the currency. It comes down to technology, resources, and political will:

• *We've got the technology to take care of our own. We've got the resources to take care of our own.*
• *All that is missing is the political will. We need democracy to quicken the will of our policy makers.*

The currency-issuing sovereign can afford to buy anything for sale in its own currency. *Duh!* Government can no more run out of money than can the scorekeeper at Fenway Park run out of runs to award the Boston Red Sox. The Fed cannot run out of reserves and banks cannot run out of deposits.
End of story.

E. MMT's Alternative Framing on Inflation

One of the biggest fears about government spending is that it can cause inflation. Let's take a deeper dive into the topic, and provide a way to reframe our views of it.

The question is not about affordability but rather concerns effects on the value of the currency and impacts on the pursuit of private interest. As Stephanie Kelton[4] says, cash registers do not discriminate: they do not care whether that dollar comes from government spending or private spending. If something is in scarce supply, more purchases of it by either government or private buyers might push up the price.

However, government purchases need to be, and can be, planned to avoid undesired crowding out and price pressures. This is more difficult for the private sector to do – since firms are in competition with one another, and "winning" a bidding war can be part of the struggle to come out on top. Government can, and should, consider the national consequences of its actions.

Where the public purpose trumps the private purpose (say, use of rubber in World War II), government has a number of options to reduce price pressure, including promotion of patriotic savings to reduce consumption, wage and price controls, and rationing. It also has the big gun: taxes. An excise tax raises the cost to private buyers; an income tax reduces disposable income to free up production for the public purpose. In those cases, the tax hike keeps the currency strong. It is needed not to "pay for" the government spending, but to avoid the crippling effects of high inflation. It provides space for government spending so that it won't worsen inflation pressures (if they exist).

Progressive taxes are justified on the basis that higher-income people pose a greater inflation threat when supplies are scarce than do low-income people. Cash registers don't discriminate – but rich folk take more dollars to market, and their spending cannot be planned, budgeted, coordinated in the way that government spending can. And spending by the rich is largely discretionary, not essential to daily life. Indeed, as one group of rich folk ramps up conspicuous consumption, other rich folk take up the challenge – that is called "keeping up with the Joneses."[5] And so do the non-rich, trying to keep up with the Kardashians. While it is true that the mega-rich do not spend a large portion of their mega-riches, they buy the more technologically advanced "toys" that use the highest-skilled labor and the most environmentally destructive production processes. Think private jets and oil-tanker-sized yachts. Their purchases are more inflationary than raising the demand by regular folk for mass-produced goods for general consumption.

When resources are scarce, taxes on the rich need to be raised to protect the currency.[6] We don't tax the rich to "pay for" government spending. Government is not in the position of Robin Hood, robbing rich folks to provide for the poor. And we should never limit the taxes on the rich to what we spend on the poor. We should tax the rich until they are no longer too rich.

As Stephanie Kelton puts it: money doesn't grow on rich people. We can keystroke the bank accounts of the poor so that they won't be poor. We increase taxes on the rich when their spending threatens our currency with inflation. Or if their riches threaten our democracy – which is the greatest threat.

If there's no inflation danger, and no democracy threat, there is no point in taxing the rich before keystroking the poor. Linking the two operations only reduces public support for helping the poor. And it's confusing and operationally wrong – except in the unlikely event that all resources are already fully utilized. Progressives must stop linking the two – that only plays into the hands of the conservatives. Progressives should instead focus on taxing the rich to reduce inequality and the threat to democracy.

The rich also are much more likely to endanger the currency's value by pulling out of the domestic currency and running to safe havens at the first sign of inflation (as they did in Argentina, creating pressures on the currency that raise inflation fears and fuel a cascading run out of pesos and into dollars). We need progressive income and inheritance taxes to protect our currency from antisocial behavior by the rich. (And we might need capital controls, too, to prevent their runs to tax havens.)

There is also a strong argument for using taxes on the rich – especially capital gains taxes – to discourage sins of various kinds. The sin of speculative excess. The sin of usury (collecting interest income). The sin of conspicuous consumption of prestige goods and services. And the sin of excess inequality. An ideal sin tax raises no revenue because it eliminates sin. While we cannot achieve that ideal, we can make sin less enjoyable. And very costly. Raise the costs of sin by taxing the dangerous activities that rich folk favor: speculation, environmental destruction, "inversions" (moving corporate headquarters offshore to escape regulations and taxation), and conspicuous consumption.

It is fitting that those who already enjoy all the benefits of life at the top ought to suffer more when they are sinful. Don't tax the sin of the worker who enjoys the occasional six-pack of brew. Go after the real sinners – those with the wherewithal to engage in truly antisocial sinning – speculative and consumption excess.

Our favored inflation themes so far:

- *We use taxes to keep our currency strong.*
- *We raise taxes when speculative excess threatens the value of our currency.*
- *Once full employment is approached, either taxes need to be raised or government spending needs to be reduced to avoid inflationary pressures.*

F. MMT's View of Government Deficits

Let's reframe our story about government deficits. As conventionally defined, a deficit means that government has spent more *into* the economy than it has taxed *out of* the economy. We add that to our savings. Government normally lets us use those savings to buy safe treasury bonds – that earn interest so that our savings continue to grow.

Government spending greater than taxing should not be called a "deficit"; rather, it is government's contribution to our savings; and government bonds are not "debt" we owe; rather, they are our net financial wealth.

- *Government spending in excess of taxes increases our savings.*

Deficits and debts are bad framing; saving and wealth are good framing.

The clock that used to sit in Times Square doesn't record our national government's debt; instead it shows our net financial wealth. Presidents Obama and Trump and Biden added trillions to our financial wealth, making up for some of the losses Wall Street and COVID-19 imposed on us. Their successors in the White House will do the same. Thanks, Uncle Sam!

- *Government bonds add to our wealth.*

Of course, as discussed earlier, government can spend too much – even if it balances its budget. It might not leave sufficient resources to promote the private purpose. It might cause inflation and currency depreciation. But there is no automatic causal sequence running directly from a deficit to inflation. Indeed, to a large extent the government's *ex post* budgetary outcome is not discretionary as it depends on the nongovernment sector's actions.

In fact, we cannot know whether a government is "running a deficit" until the end of the accounting period – when we total up all spending and taxing over the period so that we can calculate the difference between the two. There's no such thing as "deficit spending" – all government spending looks the same and takes the form of keystroking credits; all taxing looks the same and takes the form of keystroking debits. The deficit exists only *ex post*.

We should never use the term "deficit spending," not only because it is bad framing but also because there is no such thing. At the aggregate level, a government deficit creates (and is identically equal to) a nongovernment surplus; and a government surplus creates a nongovernment deficit. The government's budget can "balance" (government spending equals taxes) only if the nongovernment sector's budget "balances" (nongovernment spending equals income).

The nongovernment sector's balance is complexly determined (and indeed depends partly on the government's actions) but we can take it as at least somewhat discretionary. To the extent that the nongovernment sector (which includes the domestic private sector plus the "rest of the world") exercises discretion over its budget it means the government's budgetary outcome is not discretionary.

Let's repeat that: if we believe that the nongovernment sector has discretion over its budgetary outcome (i.e. whether to save or to spend more than its income), then we believe the government does not have discretion over its deficit. The government and nongovernment are thus inextricably bound in an inescapable balance. It makes no sense to talk about a government deficit as either imbalanced or unsustainable.

A government deficit will result if the nongovernment sector has a surplus – a perfect balance – and can persist as long as the nongovernment sector wills it to be so – a perfectly sustainable balance. Balances balance!

Of course they do.

- **Balances balance.** A theme that bears repeating.

Calls to cut the government's debt are, equivalently, by identity, calls to cut our net financial wealth. Fiscal Austerians are, by definition, wealth destroyers. And they are not just any wealth destroyers: they destroy the safest and most liquid kind of wealth we can hold – government IOUs.

- **Our meme: fiscal austerity destroys our financial wealth.**

We like it when the government owes us. Why on earth do the Austerians want to turn the tables, reducing the number of "Government Owes Me's"? Would they be happier if we all owed the government? Holding a Government Owes Me is like holding a "Get out of jail free" card – if worse comes to worst, I can pay my taxes or other bills and stay out of jail.

Deficit cutters are profit destroyers, too. As we know, government deficits mean nongovernment surpluses for households and for firms. In the case of firms, that is gross profits (receipts less spending).[7] Cutting deficits means cutting profits.

- *Our meme: deficit hawks are profit destroyers. They are unwitting enemies of capitalism.*

MMT recognizes the important role that government plays in protecting profits. Budget deficits mean private profits.

What's wrong with that?

In fact, government spending doesn't take money out of our pockets – it fills our pockets!

- *Another meme: government spending fills our pockets with money!*

Is it really moral to take money out of the pockets of hard-working Americans so that Uncle Sam can run a surplus?

MMT doesn't think so.

G. Why Is Money So Difficult to Discuss?

In a word, money is a *scary* topic.

Certainly there is no other economic topic that is so closely tied to morality. We pass moral judgments on those who have "too little" as well as those who have "too much." And, yet, you've probably never met anyone who has just the right amount.

We commonly label someone who spends "wastefully" as having "more money than brains." We do not want to be a "spendthrift" – saving money is universally regarded as wise – and, yet, one who "hoards" money is derided as a miser. We all remember poor old penny-pinching Scrooge, who had to have the living daylights scared out of him by the Ghost of Christmas Past before he realized the error of his ways.

Sigmund Freud linked money to feces, in particular likening the love of gold to a baby's obsession with poop: today's gold bug is the adult version of the baby who cannot let go of his poop. Canadian economist Ted Winslow argues that Freud had a big impact on John Maynard Keynes's views on the irrational and ultimately dangerous "love of money."[8]

Keynes's biographer, Lord Robert Skidelsky, emphasizes that the "love of money" (commonly cited as the root of all evil) is *morally* inefficient (representing the objectless pursuit of wealth for wealth's own sake) and *economically* inefficient (the psychology of the miser prevents him from actually using his money – which depresses demand).[9]

It is Scrooge's love of money that keeps the Cratchit family too poor to enjoy Christmas, which in turn robs the merchants of potential Christmas sales. Remember also that Scrooge refuses to offer coins to poor beggars, arguing that they are better off dead, to reduce the surplus population.[10] Compare that with the popular view of charity in the Depression-era expression (and song) "brother, can you spare a dime?" – when times were bad for almost everyone, such handouts were viewed favorably.

These extremes reflect our schizophrenic attitudes toward those without money: our charitable selves want to help, but our coldly rational selves worry that "misguided" charity encourages sloth.

It is said that money makes the world go round, but it is also said that money cannot buy happiness – or, at least according to The Beatles, it cannot buy love. While evidence suggests that those who win big lotteries end up no happier than those who buy tickets but do not win,[11] other studies show that happiness does tend to rise with increasing money income.[12]

Still, there seems to be a paradox: while richer communities are happier than poor ones, for individuals more money is not necessarily a path to greater happiness. As your income increases, you move into more upscale neighborhoods, where your neighbors also have more income – so you are no better off *relative to your (new) neighbors*. The problem you face is that no matter how much you have of it (money, that is), someone has more.

So as an individual moves up the social ladder, more money doesn't make her happier. However, if we compare measures of happiness across different communities we do tend to find a correlation between money income and happiness. It seems that two ways in which money *does* buy happiness are through more human connections (the poor are typically lonelier) and through ability to "buy" time by hiring others to do chores.

Money may not buy you happiness (or love), but having more money makes it easier to rent it (happiness or love)!

However, even on this score we have our qualms. It is considered fine to "rent" someone to wash dishes, cut hair, or even care for one's child, but it is not OK to "rent" someone to provide sexual pleasure. And context matters: it is perfectly fine to pay a dental hygienist to clean your teeth *at the dentist's office*, but most people would recoil in shock if you reported that you had hired someone to brush your teeth every night before bedtime – unless you have a disability that prevents you from doing so yourself.

It is not just "wasteful" spending of money that we abhor, for we fear the corrupting uses to which money might be put. Hence, in Western societies (at least) it is not considered appropriate to offer gifts of money to clerks at the Department of Motor Vehicles to speed up the vehicle registration process. Nor is it acceptable to buy votes or judicial decisions, or to pay police to look the other way when crimes are committed. Nor, generally, to sell babies or organs to obtain money. Similarly, we distrust those who are "in it only for the money," as well as those who would "do anything for a buck." We want people to "earn" the money they get, but we proscribe many possible avenues as unacceptable.

Keynes emphasized the existential conflict raised in an economy organized around "making money": the love of money drives our economy, which helps to provide the required material comfort necessary to live "wisely, agreeably, and well," but the love of money is also a neurosis because there can never be a point of satiation.[13] The fetish for hoarding money plus excessive inequality that has put most of the nation's money in the hands of the rich – who save, rather than spend – generate low sales for our nation's producers and few jobs for our unemployed.

As Keynes put it:

> We used to believe that modern capitalism was capable, not merely of maintaining the existing standards of life, but of leading us gradually into an economic paradise where we should be comparatively free from economic cares. Now we doubt whether the business man is leading us to a destination far better than our present place. Regarded as a means he is tolerable; regarded as an end he is not so satisfactory. One begins to wonder whether the material advantages of keeping business and religion in different compartments are sufficient to balance the moral disadvantages.[14]

We tolerate the "immoral" pursuit of money to the extent that it allows us to live well, but we increasingly doubt that the rat race money's pursuit has created leads to paradise. In another essay, Keynes foresaw an alternative path:

> When the accumulation of wealth is no longer of high social importance, there will be great changes in the code of morals ... The love of money as a possession – as distinguished from the love of money as a means to the enjoyments and realities of life – will be recognised for what it is, a somewhat disgusting morbidity, one of those semi-criminal, semi-pathological propensities which one

hands over with a shudder to the specialists in mental disease.[15]

That stinging indictment of the love of money – as "semi-criminal, semi-pathological" – is much harsher than Freud's analogy to the baby's love of poop!

7

MMT and Policy

In this final chapter we discuss MMT and policy, assessing MMT's impact and its main policy proposals.

A. What Is MMT's State of Play in Policy-Making Circles?

Over the past couple of years, MMT has been in the headlines. At first, it was mostly "bad press," with pundits and politicians dismissing it as "crazy talk."[1] There have been four (yes, four!) resolutions in the House and Senate condemning MMT as a threat to the nation – admittedly, all pushed by Republicans.[2]

However, after the pandemic hit, MMT was embraced as emergency policy to quickly inject five trillion dollars of "stimulus" into the economy.[3] While still considered dangerous by many, this was seen as a necessary response to save the economy from the ravages of COVID-19. The notion was that once the recession's trough was reached, sane policy would return.

President Biden, however, seemed to recognize that the new normal will not look like your grandad's normal. We face multiple pandemics: mutating viruses, climate change, intransigent poverty and inequality, a healthcare system that did not live up to the COVID-19 challenge and that is ill-prepared for the next health crisis, inadequate access to affordable higher education, an antiquated infrastructure, and a climate-driven refugee crisis. He also recognizes that tackling these comes with a high price tag – trillions of dollars. Yet surprisingly – for the first time in nearly three generations – President Biden was not completely stymied by the cost. He was the first president to clearly embrace the reality that the US can and should spend trillions of dollars to "build back better."

Unfortunately, he resurrected the idea of "pay-fors" linked to that spending – MMT was only for relief packages, not for "building back better" – building back better requires tax hikes to match the spending.[4] The "balanced budget" view is enshrined in Congressional policy, too, due to the 2010 Statutory Pay-As-You-Go (PAYGO) Act and the 2011 Budget Control Act that essentially require any fiscal policy increasing spending or lowering taxes to be "offset" by other changes to spending or taxes.

But tying tax hikes to spending is like tossing barbells to a drowning swimmer – the spending bill will drown in opposition to tax hikes.

With MMT in the headlines, one of the questions always raised by reporters is this: has MMT made any headway in Washington? Except on the fringes – for example, Congresswoman Alexandria Ocasio-Cortez and a few others have invoked MMT to reject the "pay-for" game – MMT appears to have been a one-hit wonder, used only to justify the COVID-19 relief.[5] Yet there is some evidence that leads to a more optimistic assessment of MMT's success.

In Fall 2019 I was invited by Representative John Yarmuth's (Democrat from Kentucky) office to testify on budget deficits before the House Budget Committee – that he headed.[6] Previous to and after the hearing I was told by the Congressman as well as his staff that at least the

Democratic side of the Committee was actively consider-
ing the MMT approach to fiscal policy.

I was also asked to make a long presentation to the
Congressional Budget Office's (CBO's) Macroeconomic
Analysis section that is responsible for providing long-
term budget and economic projections to Congress. They
specifically wanted me to address the implications for the
trajectory of interest rates and the burden and sustaina-
bility of that borrowing through time. They warned me
that they use the ridiculous infinite-horizons, intergenerational approach popularized by Larry Kotlikoff.[7] But they
assured me that the audience was interested in the MMT
approach and that the reception would be cordial. The
questions were indeed serious and respectful. The CBO
also asked Stephanie Kelton, a prominent MMT proponent, to give a presentation.

However, the best evidence that MMT is making inroads
is the astonishing interview that Representative Yarmuth
gave to CNN.[8] The context for the interview was the
prospect for President Biden's 2022 budget request, which
contained his proposals for "building back bigger." The
interview is a breath of fresh air and his penetrating focus
on the issues that matter represents a breakthrough. Can
the long nightmare of fiscal austerity be coming to an end?

Congressman Yarmuth nicely summarized the main
understanding he developed of MMT:

> Historically, what we've always done is said, "What can
> we *afford* to do?" And that's not the right question. The
> right question is, "*What do the American People need us
> to do?*" And *that* question becomes the first question. Once
> you answered *that*, then you say, "*How do you resource
> that need?*"

And to clarify what he meant by "resource" he focused on
"capacity."

> So, for instance, there is a $225 billion investment in child-
> care in the American Families Plan. But, you can't just say

we're going to give $225 billion to people to pay for their childcare, because there's not enough capacity ... So what you *have to* do, is spend part of that money on *building capacity* so that there is enough childcare to actually service the people who need it.

This is precisely the MMT view: rather than focusing on possible budget deficits, the CBO should be focused on increased demand for resources that might cause inflation. But, wait a minute, said the reporter – "We can just print more money and there are no consequences?" Yarmuth replied:

There could be consequences, if there is too much inflation. So, let me give you a hypothetical. We could say that, "We're going to give every American family a $200,000 voucher to buy a house." We could create the money to do that, but what would happen? Well, there is not enough housing, so the prices of existing houses would go through the roof – no pun intended! And again, you'd be creating a false promise. Meanwhile, you'd drive up the housing market to unsustainable levels. So, there is a limit as to how much money we can inject into the economy.

That is, without causing inflation. The problem is not the "money" but rather the demand on resources. The key is to ramp up capacity as we "rebuild" our economy along socially and environmentally sustainable paths, and to phase in the spending on a pace with growth of capacity. Yarmuth continued:

If you are going to spend money at the federal level, if you're going to make investments, they need to be meaningful and important investments. And they have to actually add to the economic capacity of the economy ... We can't just throw money at worthless projects.

He believed that Biden's proposals would increase capacity, attenuating inflation pressure. In response to questions about spending trillions of dollars, Yarmuth argued:

We can afford it, because we determine how much money is in the system – at the federal level. The federal government is not like any other user of currency, not like any household, any business, any state or local government. We issue our own currency, and we can spend enough to meet the needs of the American people – the only constraint being that *we do* have to worry about inflation from that spending.

As every American should know, this right of currency issue was provided to Congress by the US Constitution. But won't the government eventually exhaust its fiscal capacity? A caller commented: "I do agree there is certainly a difference between households and the government itself. However, the government does have limits. Because the government doesn't have any more money than The People have. There are limited resources." Yarmuth responded:

Let me go back to [your] comment . . . "We don't have any more money than The People have." Yes we do.
     We do have the printing presses. I hate to use that term – "printing money" – but we do. And if you think about it, we have been accumulating debt in the United States, for most of our 230-year history.[9] How did we do that? That's because the government issued a lot of money, over time, and nobody has ever been asked to pay off any of that national debt. We've been able to finance our debt when we needed to. And I think it'll remain that way. Again, the constraint on us is rampant inflation.

This is correct: the danger is not national insolvency but excess demand on the nation's resources. Congressman Yarmuth is on the right track when he argues that there is nothing wrong with spending in excess of tax revenue – as we've done for 230 years:

And we'll continue to do that, because the needs are more than we choose to tax our citizens. And the money we have – if we relied on taxation – purely on taxation – to fund the government, then a lot of people would suffer very, very seriously, because we couldn't provide nearly the services that the American people want us to provide.

Trying to squeeze more tax revenue out of the economy would reduce private spending and increase the people's need for more government services. The answer is to spend more, without taxing more, to utilize existing idle resources and to add to the nation's capacity.

What about the mountains of government debt? Who will hold it, and who is going to pay it all back? Representative Yarmuth went on:

> Now, so many people say that we have so much debt, and our grandchildren – it is going to be on their backs, and so forth. That is *not* the way it works. And I think the American people need an education about how the monetary system *does* work.
>
> I remember going back . . . to when Paul Ryan was chair of the Budget Committee, and even before that – and all of these forecasts of gloom and doom about "Oh, we are going to accumulate so much debt, and interest rates are going to crowd out all other spending."
>
> Well, we basically doubled the national debt from the recession in 2009 until last year, before the pandemic. And none of the things that people warned would happen, happened. We didn't have inflation. We had record low interest rates, rather than higher interest rates. And the dollar was trading with normal levels, vis-a-vis other currencies.
>
> So, I think a lot of economists have begun to say "wait a minute" – "Maybe we have been thinking about debt in entirely the wrong way."

Precisely. And what about the Chinese holdings? We've borrowed so much!

> Okay, I'm glad you asked that question. China owns roughly $1 trillion, roughly, of U.S. treasuries. That's it. If they said they wanted a trillion dollars, instead of a trillion dollars of treasuries, we would put a trillion dollars on their account, and that would be fine. And they could do

with that, whatever they wanted. They could leave it here. They could take it home. We can do that with anybody.

Yarmuth assured me that others understand these points, but most are afraid to make such statements in public. MMT's followers are helping to bring these ideas into the open so that our elected representatives will have the courage to tell the truth about government spending.

B. MMT's Approach and Pay-Fors

When the pandemic hit, the Trump administration quickly pushed through relief, as did the new President Biden, without worrying about "pay-fors." In the context of the emergency, MMT was mentioned favorably as a "new" approach of "money-financed" spending (sometimes likened to Friedman's helicopter money[10]). However, as the panic faded, the mood shifted and the supposed need for "pay-fors" returned. Treasury Secretary Yellen[11] argued this is necessary if we are to go big on spending – such as for Biden's "build back better" proposals:

> [W]e do need fiscal space to be able to address emergencies, like the one that we've been in with respect to the pandemic. We don't want to use up all of that fiscal space and over the long run deficits need to be contained to keep our federal finances on a sustainable basis. So, I believe that we should pay for, pay for these historic investments.

MMT rejects these notions. There is no such thing as fiscal space in financial terms. Federal government spending is "paid for" when Treasury cuts a check, the Fed credits bank reserves, and banks credit deposit accounts. Budgetary outcomes are *ex post*, only added up later, and do not impinge on financial ability to spend. There is no such thing as "deficit spending" except as an *ex post* accounting phenomenon (at the time the spending occurs we cannot know the eventual budgetary accounting).

While Congress has imposed on itself constraints – through budgetary laws that require "budget scoring" (that is, calculating whether the deficit would go up if a spending program were to be approved), "pay-fors," and sequestration (preventing spending if it would increase the debt) – these are not really financial constraints; rather, they are political constraints. The proof is that these constraints are often vitiated when it is politically viable – such as to allow Trump's tax cuts to go through, or to provide pandemic relief checks.

Furthermore, deficits are not really discretionary, as they depend on economic performance as well as the other sectoral balances. Still, the federal government can make all payments as they come due; its balance is always sustainable in the sense that bills can be paid. There is no such thing as "keeping the powder dry" by minimizing deficits now so that we can use them later. Spending foregone today does not enable more spending later. It is simply lost forever, and we lose the production that the idle resources could have produced if employed.

What matters is resources, not money. Tackling multiple pandemics comes down to mobilizing unemployed resources, shifting those already employed, and creating new ones. How to shift resources from current use to favored uses? Taxes, postponed consumption, patriotic saving (and as well, if necessary, we can use rationing and regulations to withdraw resources from low-priority private use). These were the methods used during World War II, and were discussed by John Maynard Keynes in his little 1940 book of advice on *How to Pay for the War*. Once we've released resources, government spending allocates them as desired to achieve the public purpose.

Taxes are not for spending but can release resources for public use. To shift resources from private to public use, taxes must reduce private spending. Progressives generally prefer taxes on the rich. But how many dollars must be taxed away from the rich to reduce (private) spending by $1, releasing resources for use?

What about a *millionaire* income tax? It depends on the propensity to spend of millionaires – how many dollars must their income be reduced to release a dollar's worth of resources? It would take a lot of taxes to reduce the desire of a millionaire to buy a yacht. What about the *billionaire* wealth tax proposed by many progressives? One of the selling points often made is that the tax would be so low it wouldn't hurt – which presumably means it would not change their consumption patterns at all. Rich people are relatively few in number and have relatively low propensities to spend. To free up sufficient resources by reducing their spending might require large tax increases – and, as well, measures to reduce evasion (illegal) and avoidance (legal ways of reducing tax bills).

The favorite taxes don't measure up as a particularly effective way to release resources, and even if they did, there would be no reason to try to match revenue produced with spending planned because it could take tens of dollars of revenue to reduce private spending by a dollar.

"Pay-fors" match spending and tax revenue and may not be effective to battle inflation. To control inflation we need to match the tax take to the desired reduction of private spending. This could be less than program spending; but is likely to be much more if aimed at high-income households. The CBO should recognize this when "scoring": not all revenues are equal in terms of inflation-fighting ability.[12]

Finally, why would a balanced budget increase of taxes coincide with the desired inequality reduction? If we are serious about reducing inequality, we might need to tax the one-percenters by far more than the amount we need to spend on programs targeted to lower-income Americans – given the degree of inequality we now face.

The big concern is that undertaking a huge government spending program – Medicare for all; a Green New Deal; infrastructure to bring the US into the twenty-first century; preparing the country for the next COVID pandemic – will require so much spending that inflation is inevitable. Let's say that is correct. How can we avoid inflation? We must reduce private use of resources to make way for public use.

Broad-based but progressive taxes on consumption or income likely to be consumed are more effective at reducing private use of resources (with an exemption for lower incomes). But this would be politically unpopular and counterproductive if one of the policy goals is to reduce poverty and inequality while increasing opportunities for those of modest means. For this reason, we have advocated a temporary surcharge in the form of a broad-based tax with generous exemptions to reduce resource use as infrastructure is built.[13] We would then boost consumption once the nation's capacity is increased, for example by phasing-in ramped up Social Security payments, to begin in five years. And we'll need additional policies to increase income and wealth at the bottom.

Note, however, that all of this is contingent on resource needs. Our first, rough, estimates on a broad-based Green New Deal led us to believe that such anti-inflation measures are probably not needed. The "build back better" plans advanced by Biden may add additional pressures on resources that could require policies to relieve inflation pressure.

Probably most important is to plan and carefully phase in projects at a pace that the economy's resources can handle. This is precisely what Representative Yarmuth suggested, and it is reasonable. That does raise the scary word: planning. If the global pandemic as well as the climate catastrophe we face have taught us anything, planning cannot be a scary word anymore. The prospects before us of proceeding without planning are truly terrifying

However, it is important to note that no change of procedures is required to "finance" a major public initiative: authorize spending and the Fed and Treasury know how to "finance" it. The ultimate constraint is resources, not finance. Taxes can play a role in releasing them but are not needed for financial purposes. The budgetary outcome is neither discretionary nor worrying. It will move against the cycle and will be consistent with the financial balances of the other sectors. Interest rates are determined by Central Bank policy, not markets. Inflation can be avoided by policy focused on mobilizing resources and releasing them as necessary.

C. MMT's Policy Agenda

MMT is largely descriptive: how a sovereign currency system works. While many MMT proponents are progressive, the understanding that MMT brings to our discussion about sovereign currency can be used by centrists and conservatives. Progressive MMT proponents support policies such as the Green New Deal, Medicare-for-All, millionaire and billionaire taxes to reduce inequality, anti-trust actions to reduce price gouging, a variety of welfare programs to raise incomes at the bottom, policies to reduce racial and gender discrimination, and so on. However – and this is a big "however" – these do not necessarily follow directly from MMT.

What MMT says is that finance of such programs is not a constraint – resources are a constraint, policy is a constraint, but lack of money is not. A conservative or libertarian might argue against all these programs, even if she understands that finance is not a constraint – she simply opposes them on the grounds that the "free market" solutions are better. Note that it is probable that most right-wing politicians already understand that finance is not really a constraint. They raise the issue of finance only when it comes to progressive policy.

Conservatives rarely demand "pay-fors" when they advocate a bigger military budget for a new war; they never demand "pay-fors" when they advocate more tax cuts for the rich; they don't demand "pay-fors" when they push for more subsidies of the biggest corporations. While they might invoke the ridiculous Laffer Curve argument that tax cuts for the rich "pay for themselves" through reference to "trickle-down" economics, they are well aware that this has never worked. Tax cuts for the rich always redistribute more income and wealth to the top, and they never generate enough revenue to offset the tax cut – so the budget deficit gets bigger.

Many Republicans really hope that more military spending for wars, or tax cuts for the rich, do increase the deficit. This then gives them the excuse to cut social spending or, at least, to oppose more. It is a simple "starve the beast" strategy and everyone understands this. Unfortunately, it is mostly Democrats who play the "pay-for" game – and it has been a policy disaster for the past half century.

So we need to be clear that neither progressive nor conservative policies are necessarily supported by MMT. They are policy choices enabled by understanding that finance is not a constraint.

There are, however, three policies that do follow directly from MMT – we could say that these are the core policies that all who understand the implications of MMT ought to support. MMT is best-known for advocating the job guarantee, followed by its support for interest rate targeting by the central bank, and a floating exchange rate. Let's examine each and explain why each follows from the understanding that MMT developed. We'll take them in reverse order.

Floating exchange rates

MMT lists the following five conditions as necessary for currency sovereignty:

1. Government chooses a money of account and issues a currency denominated in that money unit.
2. Government imposes liabilities (taxes, fees, fines – and in the old days, tithes and tribute in the case of religious authorities or conquerors, respectively).
3. Government accepts its own currency in payment of those liabilities.

4. If government issues other liabilities (such as bills and bonds), those are payable in its own currency.
5. Government does not promise to redeem its own currency for precious metal or other currencies (that is, currencies issued by other authorities – usually foreign) at a fixed exchange rate.

The final condition implies a floating currency. Note that by "floating" we do not mean "free float" – that is, a "market-determined" rate. Most governments intervene in some manner or other if they believe the exchange rate is moving too much – whether appreciating or depreciating. Policies that are used include changing the interest rate target (see the next section), trade policy to impact imports and exports, and capital controls (restricting financial asset flows across borders).

The critical difference between "managing" a currency using these tools and "pegging" is that in the first case government's intervention is discretionary; but in the case of a currency peg, government commits to maintaining the fixed exchange rate. If there is pressure on it (to move in either direction), government must take action. If it cannot "redeem" its currency at the fixed price against the gold or foreign currency, it has defaulted on its promise. Even the doubt that a government can maintain the peg will lead to a run-out of the currency – that is, an attempt to convert the currency to whatever it is pegged to. This generally leads to a currency, or exchange rate, crisis with results that are often devastating.

The consequence is that the country with a pegged currency surrenders some of its domestic policy space – it needs to operate its economy so that the gold, or foreign currency, flows into the country, usually through a positive trade balance, although the flow could be due to factor payments (such as profit flows from abroad) or on the capital account (sales of financial assets). When flows turn against a country with a peg, the usual response is to adopt an austerity policy to make the population sufficiently poor that they stop buying imports, and to make domestic wages sufficiently low that exports rise. This is what we mean by a reduction of policy space: it may not be possible to pursue full employment and rising living standards at home.

Pegging a currency can be somewhat less severe than actually adopting a foreign currency – often called "dollarization," as a number of countries either formally adopted the US dollar as their currency, or have rigidly pegged to the dollar and accept it in domestic payments (even of taxes). Wynne Godley, the famous economist who developed the sectoral balance approach discussed in chapter 4, said that adopting a foreign currency is equivalent to voluntarily becoming a colony of the issuer of that foreign currency. He warned that the European nations that adopted the Euro had effectively become colonies – subjecting themselves to the whims of the European Central Bank (the issuer of the Euro). We will not go into that in detail here, but history is littered with sad stories of countries that have either "dollarized" or adopted hard pegs to the US dollar. To be fair, there are a few success stories – countries that are big exporters (Singapore, for example) have been able to adopt hard pegs but still thrive.

But, generally, adopting your own currency and letting the exchange rate float creates the most domestic policy space to pursue the public interest. While MMT doesn't insist that this is best for every country in the world, for those that can make use of policy space to raise living standards, floating the currency is best.

Interest rate targeting

MMT argues that central banks can, and do, target the overnight interest rate – in the US this is called the Fed Funds rate. Other than acting as a lender of last resort in a financial crisis, acting as the treasury's bank, operating the clearing system for checks, and possibly regulating financial institutions, interest rate targeting is the most important policy of central banks. This is no longer controversial. Twenty-five years ago, when MMT began, many thought central banks can control the money supply – and they did set money growth targets. Fortunately, none of the central banks of the major economies even pretend to do that now. It is widely accepted that central banks do not have the tools to target the money supply. They do, however, set and hit the overnight interest rate, and, indeed, can target any particular interest rate they choose. For example, they can set the interest rate on thirty-year treasury bonds simply by announcing the target rate and standing by ready to sell or buy a sufficient quantity of such bonds to hit their target. This is widely recognized today.

There is, however, controversy about where to set the overnight target, and perhaps some controversy about the utility of setting and hitting other interest rates. MMT has gained a reputation for advocating near-zero overnight rates – what came to be called ZIRP (zero interest rate policy) after the GFC when many central banks did, indeed, adopt such targets. While most economists saw this as temporary policy to deal with the crisis, MMT (following John Maynard Keynes) argued that this should be permanent policy. This helps to keep other rates low (the overnight rate target is the base rate off which other rates set), which reduces interest income (Keynes called that "euthanasia of the rentier" – advocating eliminating any interest reward to those who do not take risks) that generally flows to higher-income people. At the same time, it lowers rates on borrowing – which tends to benefit lower-income people (who are net debtors). It also can promote both private and public investment by lowering the borrowing costs of financing long-term investment projects like infrastructure.

Many MMT proponents advocate elimination of government bonds altogether. They see these as unnecessary since all government spending is "paid for" through reserve credits to bank accounts held at the central bank. Bonds are then sold to drain reserves, and to let banks and others earn interest on a risk-free asset – a claim on the sovereign government. This is unnecessary and simply provides income to the holders – mostly institutions and higher-wealth individuals. Bonds also further the myth that the sovereign government needs to "borrow" from savers to "finance" its spending – which is false, as we've explained.

Hence, many MMT proponents argue for dropping the bonds. If government wants to pay a small amount of interest on reserves, so be it. It will be seen for what it is – part of monetary policy, designed to keep overnight rates above zero. A counterargument is that there's a public purpose in paying interest to some select entities, such as pension funds, other retirement accounts, and maybe insurance companies. They can hold longer-term government bonds that make part of their portfolios risk-free, but still interest-earning. However, if this is seen to be in the public interest, bond ownership should be narrowly limited only to those kinds of institutions that serve a public interest. Again, retirement savings could be an example. Or individual savings bonds, with purchases limited to lower-income households – to use for college savings, for example. This would be part of public policy to promote and reward saving by low-income households.

Job guarantee

The final policy is by far the most important for MMT: a universal job guarantee that would provide jobs at decent pay (with benefits) for anyone who wants to work. Above, we have briefly discussed the MMT view that employment is a fundamental right, particularly in a society that believes that "he who does not work, neither shall he eat." Capitalism places a high value on income payments going to those who contribute to the production process. However, it has long entertained a false presumption that the "market" can provide jobs to all who want them. This is not, and never has been, true. Under capitalism, firms hire only the number of workers they think they need to produce the amount of output that can be sold for profit. In other words, capitalists hire workers only if they think they can profit from the employment. This always leaves a substantial part of the potential labor force unemployed.

If that were not bad enough, those left behind are those who face the most discrimination – by gender, by race, by age, by ethnic origin, and by any other distinguishing characteristics that can be discriminated against. Discrimination is practiced and perpetuated because it is profitable. By discriminating against a group, employers can not only pay them less, but can also use them to keep the wages of others lower. Such discrimination is built into the nature of capitalism – it is a "divide and rule" strategy that pits worker against worker. The threat that "the other" (the group facing discrimination because of their gender, race, etc.) might take your job keeps you, too, subservient. This threat is as old as capitalism itself.

A universal job guarantee (JG) that offers equal access, equal pay, and equal treatment can counter such discrimination. The program's wage and its benefits and working conditions will set the standard that all other employers must meet. It "levels up" by "hiring off the bottom." It takes workers "as they are," provides them with jobs and decent treatment, and forces other employers to compete.

But, also importantly from the MMT view, the JG "anchors" the currency. We know that taxes "drive the currency," creating a demand for it to pay taxes to the currency's issuer. But that does not determine the currency's value. On the margin, the currency's value is determined by what you must do to obtain it. If you need to work an hour to obtain $15, that establishes the value: one hour equals $15.

Hyman Minsky used to ask students "what is the minimum wage in the US?" A student would raise her hand and say $3.35 an hour (the legal minimum wage in the early 1980s). He'd respond: "No it isn't. If you cannot find a job, you get zero." Then he'd go on to say that if there was a JG (he called it "employer of last resort," a term left over from the Roosevelt administration), that would establish an "effective minimum wage" at whatever the program paid. And then he'd talk about the virtues of the New Deal's jobs programs, that provided jobs to millions of formerly unemployed workers.

The point is this: the JG establishes the value of an hour of labor. And helps to keep it stable through time. If wages start to rise outside the JG program, employers can always recruit out of the JG program at a wage slightly above the program wage. If it pays, for example, $15 per hour, then private employers can hire labor out of the program at, say, $15.25 an hour. This helps to dampen wage and price inflation as the economy grows. The JG "anchors" the currency – by supplying labor when the private sector needs it, and by absorbing labor when the private sector lays off workers. That ensures wages do not fall below $15 an hour (in our example), no matter how bad a recession becomes. By hiring the unemployed, the program prevents a recession from going too deep – by maintaining wages and incomes.

Economists call that an automatic stabilizer, and the JG is a strong one: it maintains employment, wages, income, prices, and consumption. Government spending on the program is automatically countercyclical, rising in a slump (workers flow into the program) and falling in a boom (workers are recruited by private employers). Exactly what we want, and automatic – it doesn't require discretionary action by politicians, which could take too long. And note, given our understanding of sovereign government finances, there is no worry about "how to pay for it" – Uncle Sam can afford it.

MMT economists have worked for a quarter century building on the ideas of Hyman Minsky to develop proposals to implement a JG. They have worked out all the details – what kinds of projects, how much to pay workers and what benefits to include, who will run the program and how it will be administered, how big it is likely to be, and how effective it will be at maintaining the value of the currency and at fighting inflation. There is no need to recount all of this, as Pavlina Tcherneva has nicely summarized most of the findings in her book.[14] Like the rest of MMT, the JG has easily withstood all the critiques that have been raised. There are a number of proposals that have already been brought to Congress, and a number of groups devoted to fighting for the JG, among which we highly recommend the National Jobs For All Network.[15]

People often ask: if we "implement" MMT, how can we be sure more government spending doesn't lead to inflation? Our answers are:

1. MMT is not something you implement – it is a description of how sovereign government really spends. It concludes that affordability is not a problem. Still, how much you spend, and what you spend on, do matter. We prefer targeted spending – to achieve the public purpose. And one of the most important public purposes is to ensure that anyone who wants to work can get a job.
2. The main spending policy we recommend is the JG. It ensures full employment – providing a job to anyone who wants one. That is as targeted as you can get. Further, it is spending that *cannot* cause inflation. It sets a "floor price" to labor, with the wage it pays anchoring wages. As per our example above: 1 hour = $15. Once everyone gets a job, government spending stops growing. If the economy picks up, workers are pulled out of the program and government spending falls. Automatically. It is an automatic stabilizer – and automatic inflation fighter. It is a "fixed price/floating quantity model" (see chapter 3) and as such cannot cause inflation.

To be sure, the JG is not the only government program. Liberals will want lots of others. Conservatives will want different ones, and maybe less government. MMT will let them negotiate all of that with the democratic process

choosing the final mix. Whatever that mix is, the JG will
ensure full employment and will exert a stabilizing force
on prices and the economy as a whole.

D. Conclusion

The monetary system is a wonderful creation. It allows
for individual choice while giving government access to
resources needed to allow it to work for us to achieve a
just society.

The monetary system spurs entrepreneurial initiative. It
finances, organizes, and distributes much of the nation's
output. It is one of the primary mechanisms used by government to accomplish the public purpose.

There could be a better way to organize production
and distribution. There could be a better way to allocate
resources between public and private. There could be a
better way to induce the private sector to serve not only its
own interest but also the public interest. But if so, we have
not yet seen it.

Until that better system comes along, we need a progressive meme for the monetary system we've got. Progressives
have been in retreat for the past half century. Yes, they've
won some battles – mostly in the social sphere. They've
lost almost all economic battles, however. At least some
of those losses are due to adoption of the wrong framing
of money.

We need to recognize that the monetary system is important. It is not merely – or even mainly – used to lubricate
exchange of goods and services. From its origins, the monetary system has played an important role in pursuit of
the public interest. It also is used in pursuit of the private
interest. And it is – especially in recent years – used by an
elite of Wall Street insiders in their own selfish interests.

To be sure, the monetary system cannot and should
not do everything. While capitalism tends to extend the
monetary sphere into an ever-larger proportion of our

social provisioning processes ("the economy"), that can be carried much too far. There are areas that need to be kept off limits, including many functions within the purview of government.

We pay our judges and lawyers but we do not want them to sell judgments to the highest bidder. We let our candidates for higher office accept campaign funds, but we do not want candidates to sell themselves to contributors.

As we push progressive memes we acknowledge that we deserve a better government than we've got – and better than we've had even when at its best. Many of those in government serve private interests, not the public interest. They've been bought and paid for.

The monetary system provides the power to do good, and the power to do bad is the other side of the coin. Still, even a largely bought and incompetent government (remember "Heckuva Job Brownie," aka Michael Brown in charge of President Bush's rescue of New Orleans after Hurricane Katrina?) is better than no government.

Even the highly suspect bailout of Wall Street in the aftermath of the GFC was better than no policy response at all. A better government can serve us better (compare the Obama administration's handling of Hurricane Sandy to Bush's handling of Katrina). Perfection is hard to achieve, but not necessary to attain some success.

Good is not the enemy of perfection.

As we've discussed, modern cognitive science teaches that we think through the use of stories that integrate words and audio-visual-sensory memories. Stories engage the reader and trigger emotional responses. Coherent narratives are easier to remember. While we might think of stories as little more than entertainment, in fact, stories help us to process, organize, and better understand the information flowing from our five senses.

Brian Boyd goes further, focusing on the evolutionary advantages that story-telling has had, arguing that "we cannot, in fact, live without stories, because they are an adaptation that has enabled our success as a species. We

enjoy them, they bring us together and foster coopera-
tion and sharing of values, they encourage attention and
empathy."[16]

We've told a different money story in this book to
reinforce the main ideas. After all, the way that we will
convince others is through story-telling. While lots of economists like to parade around with their complex math,
their models simply add a patina of sophistication to the
simple stories they tell. Stories win the debates, not math.

And we've got the better stories.

Keynes once said he hoped for the day when economists
might be thought as useful as dentists. That's a two-edged
sword. It requires first that economists actually become, as
Keynes said, as humble and as competent at their craft as
dentists are at theirs. Unfortunately, that day still resides
beyond reach. Economists are rarely humble and often
precisely wrong. Their errors do not build the confidence
that Keynes hoped for.

Further, economists are masters at putting simple
ideas into mathematically complex models that no one
can understand. This is intentional obfuscation. We hope
that this book can make a positive contribution toward
Keynes's goal of raising the reputation of the economics
profession – perhaps at least part way to the esteem in
which dentistry is held.

Notes

Preface

1 Hyman P. Minsky, *Stabilizing an Unstable Economy*, Yale University Press, New Haven and London, 1986, pp. 228 and 231.
2 L. Randall Wray, *Money and Credit in Capitalist Economies: The Endogenous Money Approach*, Edward Elgar, Aldershot, 1990.
3 L. Randall Wray, *Why Minsky Matters: An Introduction to the Work of a Maverick Economist*, Princeton University Press, Princeton and Oxford, 2015.
4 John Maynard Keynes, *A Treatise on Money*, Volumes I and II, Harcourt, Brace, New York, 1930.
5 Georg Friedrich Knapp, *The State Theory of Money*, Clifton, NY, Augustus M. Kelly, 1924 (1973).
6 L. Randall Wray (ed.), *Credit and State Theories of Money: The Contributions of A. Mitchell Innes*, Edward Elgar, Cheltenham, 2004.
7 L. Randall Wray, *Understanding Modern Money: The Key to Full Employment and Price Stability*, Edward Elgar, Cheltenham, 1998.
8 That was updated in the second edition: L. Randall Wray, *Modern Money Theory: A Primer on Macroeconomics*

for Sovereign Monetary Systems, Palgrave Macmillan, Basingstoke, 2015.

9 William Mitchell, L. Randall Wray, and Martin Watts, *Macroeconomics*, Red Globe Press, London, 2019.

1 What Is Money?

1 The word "nominal" derives from the Latin *nomen* and *nominalis* (name) and is related to the Greek word for money, *nomisma*. Outside economics, the word "nominal" is commonly used in a somewhat derogatory manner, to indicate something of inconsequential value, or something that isn't "real." For example, a popular dictionary defines the word as follows: "A nominal price or sum of money is very small in comparison with the real cost or value of the thing that is being bought or sold." https://www.collinsdictionary.com /us/dictionary/english/nominal. However, as we'll emphasize, out in the "real" economic world, value in money terms ("nominal") is exceedingly important.

2 Today there is much greater diversity, with most mortgages packaged into securities. We will stick with the simplest case here.

3 Note burning parties have become rare as few Americans now manage to pay off their mortgages before they die. However, these parties were common in the middle of the last century. Wikipedia: "The concept of a mortgage burning party was immortalized in a 1975 episode of *All In The Family*, 'Mike Makes His Move.' Mortgage burnings were also the premise of a 1977 episode of *Eight Is Enough*, 'Mortgage Burnin' Blues,' and a 1982 episode *of M*A*S*H*, 'Settling Debts'." https://en.wikipedia.org/wiki/Mortgage_burning.

4 Similarly, when the bank returns your mortgage note to you, you could frame and mount it rather than burning it. So long as you hold it, it is not your liability. You also could write a stack of IOUs and keep them in a closet, but they would become liabilities only if you issued them to others. The danger is that someone might steal your IOUs and then try to enforce them in court. One reason to burn or shred liabilities when they are returned to the issuer is to ensure that doesn't happen.

5 The US Treasury does not follow standard practice; it counts its coins as "equity" rather than as "debt"; however, equity is also on the liability side of the balance sheet so this quirk is not important.

6 From the 1930s until the early 1980s, US banks were prohibited from paying interest on demand deposits by what was known as "Regulation Q." The idea was that competition among banks for deposits drove up interest rates paid, which then encouraged banks to engage in riskier activities to increase earnings. The problem, however, was that other kinds of financial institutions innovated to offer "deposit-like" liabilities that did pay interest; this unfair competition caused "disintermediation" as depositors withdrew funds from regulated banks to earn interest at unregulated "non-bank banks" (what we now call shadow banks). Ending Regulation Q was supposed to level the playing field, letting banks also pay interest.

7 Like mortgages, credit card debt is securitized. Indeed, all kinds of debts are securitized, including student loans and car leases. This means that a bunch of debts are packaged into a "security" that is sold to investors. Payments made on the debts (e.g. the monthly mortgage or credit card payment) are paid to the investors that hold the security. The securities are supposedly safe because if a few debtors miss their payments, the vast majority will make theirs so that the security holders get paid – at least something. Effectively debts serve as a sort of collateral behind the security, and payments on those debts are the income the holder receives. The securitizer that put together the package is paid up front by the investor – they do not receive income from the debt. Banks often securitize the loans they make so that they get paid immediately and do not have to worry whether the debtors make the payments – they shift the risk to the investors in the securities.

8 Americans were not even allowed to own gold bullion, due to the Gold Reserve Act passed under President Roosevelt in 1934. President Ford changed the law in 1974, finally allowing Americans to own gold – but by that time, the US dollar was no longer convertible to gold.

9 Farley Grubb, "Colonial Virginia's Paper Money Regime, 1755–1774: A Forensic Accounting Reconstruction of

the Data," Working Paper No. 2015-11, University of Delaware Alfred Lerner College of Business and Economics, 2015. https://moodle.bard.edu/pluginfile.php/156053/mod _resource/content/1/farley%20grubb%20on%20colonial %20paper%20money.pdf.

10 Adam Smith, *The Wealth of Nations*, The Cannan Edition, Modern Library, New York, 1937, p. 312.

11 Beardsley Ruml, "Taxes for Revenue Are Obsolete," *American Affairs*, vol. 8, no. 1 (January 1946), pp. 35–9.

12 Tallies were initially issued as receipts but by the fourteenth century the exchequers issued tallies directly to creditors. In the fourteenth and fifteenth centuries, tallies accounted for the majority of receipts to the British crown. Desan links colonial use of paper notes to the British experience with tallies. Christine Desan, *Making Money: Coin, Currency, and the Coming of Capitalism*, Oxford University Press, Oxford, 2014.

13 The "score" was among the most common notches, indicating a value of 20 English pounds. We still use that term to indicate points earned in a game or on a test, to scratch or notch wood, or (less commonly) to indicate a set of twenty ("Four score and seven years ago" as President Lincoln put it in his Gettysburg Address to indicate eighty-seven years).

14 As a side note, the Bank of England was created because the king had defaulted on his tally sticks – so no one would take his IOUs. Parliament had to create a special bank to do so – the Bank of England. That was the original purpose of central banks – to accept the debt of sovereigns who were deemed to be unworthy of trust.

15 They were issued by the English crown until 1826 and finally went out in a "blaze of glory" in England in 1834. They had been stored in the Star Chamber and other parts of the House of Commons, so to save space "it was decided that they should be thrown into the heating stoves of the House of Commons. So excessive was the zeal of the stokers that the historic parliament buildings were set on fire and razed to the ground" (Glyn Davies, *A History of Money: From Ancient Times to the Present Day*, University of Wales Press, Cardiff, 1997, p. 663).

16 Technological "advances" often reduce the costs of running the payments system – but there can be drawbacks. If you go to the bank to withdraw cash to make payments, it is far less

likely that you'll end up with insufficient funds than if you write checks; and you are more likely to get deeply into debt using a credit card than you would if you exclusively rely on checks or on debit cards.

17 Yes, some see crypto coins as a replacement; these are not obligations and there is no possibility of redemption. While the "blockchain" technology may prove to be useful to prevent counterfeits and to protect data, we do not see these crypto coins as currency.

18 Remember that every "money asset" is also a "money debt." Beauty is in the eye of the beholder. From the viewpoint of the issuer, it is a debt; from that of the holder, it is an asset.

19 We won't go into detail, but the price for a bond that you sell before maturity depends on market interest rates at the time of sale. Further, in the case of bonds that are not issued by the national government, there is a risk of default: the corporation or municipality that issued the bond might go bankrupt or default on its promise to pay. Perceptions of default risk can vary over time, so if you try to sell the bond at the wrong time (i.e. when markets think the risk of default is high), you will receive a lower price. So bonds are less liquid because it can take time to convert them to cash, and there is some uncertainty over their value.

20 Technically, currency is like a consol (a "perpetual" bond that never matures, promising to pay interest "forever") that pays zero interest.

21 This is because there is "capital risk" on long-term bonds. If interest rates rise (because the central bank raises its target interest rate), long-term bond prices will fall. So to compensate their holders for the risk of that happening, these bonds need to pay a higher interest than short-term bonds, as the prices of short-term bonds will move much less when interest rates rise (as they have a shorter term to maturity). We won't go into that calculation, which, again, can be complex.

2 Where Does Money Come From?

1 In 2021, the federal government was anticipated to spend $6.8 trillion, while collecting $3.8 trillion in revenue. We will assume that 2021 is an unusual year (with revenue

averaging just $7 million a minute in large part due to the pandemic-induced slowdown of the economy) and presume it will average a higher number ($10 million a minute).

2 For a number of reasons, the treasury has maintained higher balances since the global financial crisis (GFC) of the mid-to-late 2000s – see https://fredblog.stlouisfed.org /2017/10/treasuring-cash/.

3 Since the GFC, the Fed has bought many trillions of bonds – boosting its assets to as high as $7 trillion. There truly is no limit!

4 Economists have expanded the model to include many banks, profits for firms, and interest payments. We won't go through that here.

5 A small rural bank might keep deposits in a big city bank to use for clearing – its account there is debited when one of its checks is received for clearing, or credited if it receives a check drawn on another bank.

6 Notes are issued to refill ATM machines, with reserves debited to "pay for" the cash.

7 Note the use of the term "score" again – derived from "scoring" a tally stick – that is, carving a mark to represent a value of twenty

3 Can We Have Too Much Money?

1 On a gold standard, the government promises to exchange its currency for gold at a fixed ratio. Prudence dictates limiting the issue of currency relative to the gold stock so there is always a sufficient gold supply to convert currency on demand. The ability to issue "money" in the form of convertible currency is limited.

2 Following Hyman Minsky, we will define capital development very broadly to include developing physical and human capital. Physical capital would include public infrastructure (bridges, airports, schools) and private factories and farms; human capital would include an educated and trained workforce as well as care services for the young and aged. We should also include building up the regenerative capacity of our natural world so that we can have clean air and water and avoid climate catastrophe. President Biden's 2021

"Build Back Better" plan takes a similar approach – with both physical infrastructure and social infrastructure.

3　At least, until the sovereign adopts a new currency. This does happen – although rarely in modern democratic societies. However, when a government falls and a new nation is proclaimed, it often adopts a new money of account.

4　Sometimes governments lend currency into existence. In modern economies, central banks usually do the lending, in the form of "reserves" lent to banks. Some governments also lend through their treasuries (or special entities such as the Small Business Administration in the USA) – which leads to a credit to bank reserves. Currency can get into the economy through both lending and spending.

5　Note that precisely what we want to include in our money stock is subject to debate. Countries usually adopt several different measures – in the US the two measures most commonly used are M1 (essentially cash plus checkable deposits) and M2 (essentially M1 plus less liquid time deposits). Definitions typically change over time as financial institutions innovate new kinds of financial instruments. We are not going to get deeply into the details as you can pursue this topic by reading any money and banking textbook.

6　Financial assets are someone's debts. If asset prices are falling, the debts are also falling in value – because the debtors cannot pay. This is why debts "deflate" when asset prices "deflate." See Irving Fisher, "The Debt-Deflation Theory of Great Depressions," 1933. https://fraser.stlouisfed.org/files/docs/meltzer/fisdeb33.pdf.

7　See L. Randall Wray, *Why Minsky Matters: An Introduction to the Work of a Maverick Economist*, Princeton University Press, Princeton and Oxford, 2015, for a detailed examination of Minsky's theories.

4 Balances Balance

1　This chapter draws on https://www.levyinstitute.org/pubs/wp_704.pdf, which was based on a presentation given at a conference held in Berlin in October 2011 by The Research Network Macroeconomics and Macroeconomic Policies.

2　For a critical examination of the adaptation of methods used in physics to economics, see Philip Mirowski, *More Heat than Light: Economics as Social Physics, Physics as Nature's Economics*, Cambridge University Press, Cambridge, 2011 (1989).

3 Margaret Atwood, *Payback: Debt and the Shadow Side of Wealth*, House of Anansi Press, Toronto, 2008. Yes, she is *that* Margaret Atwood, the Canadian poet, novelist, literary critic, essayist, teacher, environmental activist, and inventor who wrote *The Handmaid's Tale* and other masterpieces. Her book on debt is a fascinating and entertaining deep dive into the topic.

4 Ibid., pp. 55–6.

5 John F. Henry, "The Social Origins of Money: The Case of Egypt," in *Credit and State Theories of Money: The Contributions of A. Mitchell Innes*, ed. L. Randall Wray, Cheltenham and Northampton, Edward Elgar, 2004, pp. 70–98.

6 Philip Grierson, *The Origins of Money*, Athlone Press, London, 1977.

7 Michael Hudson, . . . *And Forgive Them Their Debts: Lending, Foreclosure and Redemption From Bronze Age Finance to the Jubilee Year*, ISLET, Dresden, 2018.

8 Frederick Soddy was an early twentieth-century physicist; he also wrote books advocating an end to the gold standard and use of the government's budget balance to counteract the business cycle. The Soddy principle posits that financial debts grow at a rate compounded by the interest rate which exceeds the capacity of the economy to grow – meaning that the debt-to-income (or debt-to-GDP) ratio will grow without limit. This is also what the Babylonians had concluded thousands of years earlier – which is why they practiced periodic debt cancellation.

9 Hudson, . . . *And Forgive Them Their Debts*.

10 Before the development of capitalism, economic growth was quite slow – almost imperceptible over one's lifetime.

11 Later we used prisons and execution exclusively for retribution – an eye for an eye, a life for a life, so that the scales would balance. We briefly experimented with the notion that prisons should reform prisoners – but as it turned out, imprisonment is not an effective way to produce good humans. Hence, we've returned to punishment. With

victims usually uncompensated for loss, there is pressure to increase the terms of punishment so that the guilty can "pay their debt to society" through suffering.

12 An institutionalist economist of great wit – known for his limericks as well as his propensity to found new subdisciplines of economics including Grants Economics, General Systems Theory, and Ecodynamics.

13 As you probably know, the US runs what is called a trade deficit. That is the main driver of foreign saving of US dollars, although the measure we use here is broader, the current account, which includes factor incomes like profits and interest. Overall, the foreign sector has consistently run a current account surplus against the US – meaning it "saves" dollars as it accumulates US dollar-denominated debt.

14 That could be avoided only if the US were to run offsetting current account surpluses – a highly unlikely scenario.

15 "15 Then the Pharisees went and plotted how to entangle him in his words. 16 And they sent their disciples to him, along with the Herodians, saying, 'Teacher, we know that you are true and teach the way of God truthfully, and you do not care about anyone's opinion, for you are not swayed by appearances. 17 Tell us, then, what you think. Is it lawful to pay taxes to Caesar, or not?' 18 But Jesus, aware of their malice, said, 'Why put me to the test, you hypocrites? 19 Show me the coin for the tax.' And they brought him a denarius. 20 And Jesus said to them, 'Whose likeness and inscription is this?' 21 They said, 'Caesar's.' Then he said to them, 'Therefore render to Caesar the things that are Caesar's, and to God the things that are God's'" (Matthew 22, English Standard Version).

16 The monetarist Milton Friedman is famous for his call on the central bank to adopt a rule for the constant rate of money supply growth; for example, the target would be for money to grow at 4 percent per year. This is supposed to be possible and would purportedly eliminate inflation. No modern central bank operating in any of the developed economies follows Friedman's recommendation any more, and the idea that a central bank can control the money supply is now regarded by central bankers as incorrect.

17 Wynne Godley, *London Review of Books*, vol. 14, no. 19 (October 8, 1992).

18 Greece tried to revolt against the Euro – but it lost.
19 See William Black, *The Best Way to Rob a Bank Is to Own One: How Corporate Executives and Politicians Looted the S&L Industry*, University of Texas Press, Austin, 2005.

5 Life Is Full of Trade-Offs

1 Thorstein Veblen, *Theory of the Leisure Class*, London, Prometheus Books, 1998 (1898), pp. 389–90.
2 Actually, MMT has the explanation: national savings rates of the private sector depend on sectoral balances. Asian countries typically have high current account surpluses and some also have high government deficits. Together, these ensure high surpluses of the domestic private sector. Ergo, high savings rates (the ratio of saving to GDP is high) in Asia.
3 Robert J. Gordon, *The Rise and Fall of American Growth: The U.S. Standard of Living Since the Civil War*, Princeton University Press, Princeton, 2017. The special century is 1870–1970; Gordon's argument is that innovations in the first half of that (1870–1920) paid off with much higher productivity and faster, sustained, economic growth in the second half (1920–70). He credits government spending for keeping aggregate demand high enough to make use of the greater productive capacity.
4 "The world is my oyster" derives from a play by Shakespeare, *The Merry Wives of Windsor*, where Falstaff says: "I will not lend thee a penny," to which Pistol replies: "Why, then, the world's mine oyster, which I with sword will open."
5 Of course, as discussed earlier, your choices are constrained by your budget constraint. The important point is that you will reach your budget constraint before you are satiated – you still want *more* but are consuming as much as you can given your income.
6 The brilliant heterodox economist Duncan Foley proposes an alternative test. He recounts a scene in the documentary made by D. J. Pennebaker about Bob Dylan, in which Dylan implores a reporter to tell the truth (Duncan Foley, "The Ins and Outs of Late Twentieth-Century Economics," Department of Economics, Barnard College, Columbia

University, New York, NY 10027 [May 25, 1998]). Foley reports: "The reporter asks what 'the truth' would be, and Dylan says, 'a picture on one page of David Rockefeller coming out of Chase Manhattan Bank, and on the opposite page of a bum vomiting in the gutter.' As I reflected on this remark in the context of economic theory, it occurred to me that it would be possible to make an incomplete ordering of the consumption bundles of two individual agents without assuming cardinality of utility by asking whether each agent's bundle was preferred to the other's in her own preference ordering. If each preferred the other's, a Pareto-improving exchange would be possible; if each preferred her own, there would be no ground for regarding either as better off; but if both preferred one agent's bundle, we could rigorously regard that agent as the better-off of the two." So in our example, if the poor guy prefers the lifestyle of the rich guy, while the rich guy also prefers his consumption bundle over the poor guy's meager consumption, then it makes sense to redistribute from the rich to the poor.

7 Karl Marx had called this a "reserve army of the unemployed," maintained by capitalists to keep labor subservient. Not surprisingly, conventional economists did not cite Marx – but their policy was designed to create his reserve army of the unemployed.

6 The MMT Alternative Framework for Policy

1 See especially David Graeber's book, *Debt: The First 5000 Years*, Melville House, Brooklyn, NY, 2011.

2 Note that we are not claiming that all economists are conservative. We are talking about the framing usually adopted by economics and economists. Lakoff is an expert on linguistics. See George Lakoff, *The ALL NEW Don't Think of an Elephant! Know Your Values and Frame the Debate*, Chelsea Green, Vermont, 2014. We will simplify his theories.

3 The title of a song by Bruce Springsteen from his *Wrecking Ball* album (2012); it was used throughout the presidential campaign of President Obama.

4 An American economist, MMT proponent, and advisor to

Senator Bernie Sanders. See Stephanie Kelton, *The Deficit Myth: Modern Monetary Theory and the Birth of the People's Economy*, Public Affairs, New York, 2020.

5 Thorstein Veblen's 1898 *Theory of the Leisure Class* (London, Prometheus Books, 1998) popularized the concepts of "conspicuous consumption" (also called "keeping up with the Joneses") and "invidious distinction" ("green with envy").

6 Although we must remember the points raised above: the propensity to consume of the rich is relatively low, so rate hikes must be large to have much impact; and if rising inflation is truly a threat, we'll probably need to tax middle incomes, too.

7 We could get into the Kalecki profits equation – that demonstrates mathematically that government deficits add to profits (all else equal) – but we shall hold off on technical details.

8 E. G. Winslow, "Keynes and Freud: Psychoanalysis and Keynes's Account of the 'Animal Spirits' of Capitalism," *Social Research*, vol. 53, no. 4 (Winter 1986), pp. 549–78.

9 Robert Skidelsky, *Keynes: The Return of the Master*, Public Affairs, New York, 2009, p. 142.

10 This was probably a swipe by Charles Dickens at the Malthusian theory that helping the poor only encourages them to have more (poor) children.

11 http://www.bbc.com/future/story/20130326-why-money -cant-buy-you happiness.

12 https://www.theguardian.com/commentisfree/2016/may/17 /money-cant-buy-happiness-wishful-thinking.

13 Skidelsky, *Keynes*, p. 144.

14 https://gutenberg.ca/ebooks/keynes-essaysinpersuasion/key nes-essaysinpersuasion-00-h.html#Short_View.

15 https://gutenberg.ca/ebooks/keynes-essaysinpersuasion/key nes-essaysinpersuasion-00-h.html#Economic_Possibilities.

7 MMT and Policy

1 Bill Gates called it "crazy talk" (https://www.nytimes .com/2019/04/05/business/economy/mmt-wall-street.html); Larry Fink called MMT "garbage" (Peggy Collins, "BlackRock CEO Larry Fink Says Modern Monetary

Theory Is 'Garbage,'" *Bloomberg*, March 7, 2019. https://
www.bloomberg.com/news/articles/2019-03-07/blackrock
-s-ceo-fink-says-modern-monetary-theory-is-garbage);
Ken Rogoff called it "nonsense" (Ken Rogoff, "Modern
Monetary Nonsense," *Project Syndicate*, March 4, 2019.
https://www.project-syndicate.org/commentary/federal
-reserve-modern-monetary-theorydangers-by-kenneth-r
ogoff-2019-03?barrier=accesspaylog); Summers claimed
that the left's "embrace" of MMT would be a "disaster"
(Lawrence H. Summers, "The Left's Embrace of Modern
Monetary Theory is a Recipe for Disaster," *Washington
Post*, March 4, 2019. https://www.washingtonpost.com
/opinions/the-lefts-embrace-of-modern-monetary-theory
-is-a-recipe-for-disaster/2019/03/04/6ad88eec-3ea4-11e9
-9361-301ffb5bd5e6_story.html); and the Nikkei Staff
Writers reported that the Bank of Japan rejects MMT
(Nikkei Staff Writers, "Growing Modern Monetary Theory
Debate Rattles Japan Officials," *Nikkei Asia*, May 28, 2019.
https://asia.nikkei.com/Economy/Growing-Modern-Moneta
ry-Theory-debate-rattles-Japan-officials).
2 The last of these four House resolutions is here: https://hern
.house.gov/uploadedfiles/mmt_-_117th.pdf; Bernie Sanders
stood up to block the most recent Senate resolution: https://
www.c-span.org/video/?c4962723/user-clip-bernie-sanders
-debates-mike-braun-mmt; and a previous Senate version is
here: https://www.congress.gov/116/crec/2019/05/01/CREC
-2019-05-01-pt1-PgS2576.pdf.
3 Congress appropriated about $5 trillion for COVID-19
relief, through the Coronavirus Aid, Relief, and Economic
Security (CARES) Act (March 2020, $2.2 trillion), as part
of the Consolidated Appropriations Act of December
2020 ($900 billion), and then the American Rescue Plan
Act (March 2021, $1.9 trillion). See Yeva Nersisyan and
L. Randall Wray, "Can Biden Build Back Better? Yes, If He
Abandons Fiscal 'Pay-Fors'," Levy Institute Public Policy
Brief No. 155, Annandale-on-Hudson, NY: Levy Economics
Institute of Bard College, 2021.
4 Ibid.
5 See https://www.bloomberg.com/news/articles/2021-07-23
/modern-monetary-theory-embrace-of-big-budget-deficits-d
oesn-t-mean-mmt-has-won?sref=VvJhl47t and also https://

www.nytimes.com/2019/04/05/business/economy/mmt-wall
-street.html for a discussion of MMT's impact on thinking about policy. For a more optimistic view, also see Von
Drehle (David Von Drehle, "So Long, Balanced Budgets:
Everyone's Into Endless Spending Now," *Washington Post*,
April 7, 2020. https://www.washingtonpost.com/opinions
/so-long-balanced-budgets-everyones-into-endless-spending
-now/2020/04/07/1e2d49f2-78f5-11ea-9bee-c5bf9d2e3
288_story.html), who argued that "everyone's into endless spending now"; and Greifeld (Robert Greifeld, "Op-
Ed: Pandemic Moves Modern Monetary Theory from the
Fringes to Actual U.S. Policy," *CNBC*, April 29, 2020.
https://www.cnbc.com/2020/04/29/op-edpandemic-moves-
modern-monetary-theory-from-the-fringes-to-actual-us-poli
cy.html), who argues that actual policy is following MMT.

6   The announcement is here: https://budget.house.gov/legisla
tion/hearings/reexamining-economic-costs-debt;   written
testimony is here: http://www.levyinstitute.org/publications/
statement-of-senior-scholar-l-randall-wray to the house-
budget-committee; the video is here: https://www.you
tube.com/watch?v=46xhX-GGJWol.

7   For a thorough critique of this methodology see James K.
Galbraith, L. Randall Wray and Warren Mosler, "The Case
Against Intergenerational Accounting: The Accounting
Campaign Against Social Security and Medicare," Levy
Institute Public Policy Brief No. 98, Annandale-on-Hudson,
NY: Levy Economics Institute of Bard College, February
2009.

8   https://www.c-span.org/video/?512625-5/washington-jour
nal-rep-john-yarmuth-d-ky-discusses-president-bidens-
fy-2022-budget-request. Faithfully transcribed by Kelly
Gerling and available here: https://medium.com/@KellyGer
ling/rep-john-yarmuth-d-ky-03-talks-about-mmt-to-answer-
what-do-the-american-people-need-us-to-do-da9a4f84ec98.

9   The federal government debt ratio has grown at a rate that
averaged 1.82 percent per year between 1791 and 2018. If
the ratio has grown at a rate approaching 2 percent per year
for over 200 years, one could reasonably anticipate that
it will continue to grow – without disaster. See L. Randall
Wray, "Testimony: Statement of Senior Scholar L. Randall
Wray to the House Budget Committee, US House of

Representatives. Reexamining the Economic Costs of Debt,"
November 2019. https://www.levyinstitute.org/publications
/statement-of-senior-scholar-l-randall-wray-to-the-house
-budget-committee.

10 Willem H. Buiter, "The Helicopters Are Coming," Project
Syndicate, March 26, 2020. https://www.project-syndicate
.org/commentary/helicopter-money-coronavirusresponseby
-willem-h-buiter-1-2020-03?barrier=accesspaylog.

11 Janet Yellen in "Meet the Press – May 2, 2021". https://
www.nbcnews.com/meet-the-press/meet-press-may-2-2021
-n1266079.

12 See Nersisyan and Wray, "Can Biden Build Back Better?"

13 Yeva Nersisyan and L. Randall Wray, "Can We Afford the
Green New Deal?" Levy Institute Public Policy Brief No.
148, Annandale-on-Hudson, NY: Levy Economics Institute
of Bard College, 2020.

14 Pavlina Tcherneva, *The Case for a Job Guarantee*, Polity,
Cambridge, 2020.

15 National Jobs For All Network. https://njfac.org.

16 Sue Bond, "Review – *On the Origin of Stories: Evolution,
Cognition, and Fiction* by Brian Boyd (Belknap Press of
Harvard University Press, 2009)," *Metapsychology*, vol. 13,
no. 41 (October 6, 2009). http://metapsychology.mentalhelp
.net/poc/view_doc.php?type=book&id=5171.

Index

Page numbers in *italics* denotes a table or figure.